Herein contains truth

MW01233842

VICTORIOUS LIVING

through

HEAVEN'S
❧ GREAT ❧
HOPE

*A divine relevation of HOPE
granted for overcoming in challenging times*

Dr. Victor Morgan, Th.D.

SECOND EDITION

ISBN: 978-0-9974942-3-5

Library of Congress Control Number: 2016941574

Published by

P.O. Box 2839, Apopka, FL 32704

Printed in the United States of America

Dedication

This book is dedicated to my two little men, my grandsons Collin and Nathan.

My trust is that when I am promoted to heaven, you will hold dear the content of this book and treat it as a treasure of insightful wisdom for your times. I pray, by the grace of God, you will have the heart to walk in the council contained in this writing and will have the courage to share it with others who will be in desperate need of genuine hope.

But as for now, I take my hat off in honor of you, my two little amazing men. God bless you, sons.

With love,
Your Grandfather

Table of Contents

Introduction

This is a book of HOPE. Hope has great power, which serves as "*an anchor of the soul, both sure and steadfast*" (Hebrews 6:19). In turbulent times, many will seek a safe harbor to secure their souls. Most people will never find it. What will hold Christians stable in stormy times is HOPE. HOPE is a gracious gift, given by God to His beloved children for such times as these that are upon us.

The Book of Daniel (12:1) tells us of these days: "*There shall be* [in the near future] *a time of trouble, such as never was.*" Daniel says, that as we draw closer to the end of time, "*many shall run to and fro*" (*v.* 4). See, in times of great trouble many will run here and there, seeking a safe harbor. However, God gives *His* children divine stability. Our loving, heavenly Father gives us HOPE! In this book, we will explore many facets of this great gift of HOPE and the absolute necessity of it for surviving the coming storm.

We are facing a time upon earth in which a directive of Jesus must be fulfilled by His Church. Jesus said for us to pray, "*Thy kingdom come*" (Matthew 6:10). He told us to "*seek…first the kingdom*" (*v.* 33). The Greek word translated "first" here means first in importance, primary, foremost, or chiefly. Hence, we are to seek, more than ever, the Kingdom of God above all else.

Jesus also declared that His Kingdom is not of the earth or of this present world. He said neither is it observed (seen) with the natural physical eye of man. His Kingdom is of another realm, or world, which is above this earth. The Kingdom of the Lord is something we must begin to press into as never before. We will not be fully in it until we walk through the pearly gates of heaven. However, we are to begin entering the Kingdom of heaven here and now, through our communion with the Holy Spirit. We are to seek the Kingdom, above all else, as Jesus instructed us to do— *"seek ye first* [or foremost] *the kingdom of God"… "for it is the Father's good pleasure to give you the kingdom"* (Matthew 6:33 and Luke 12:32).

As we seek the Kingdom, through the Holy Spirit, we begin to get glimpses of it and have experiences in it. The Holy Spirit gives us foretastes of the coming Kingdom of God, thereby, giving us the assurance of its reality. As this occurs, we begin to develop a greater yearning and a HOPE for the day when we will walk on the streets of gold, along with the patriarchs of old and the holy angels, bowing before the throne of the Father in perfected praise and adoration.

There is a great visitation of God coming to the Church in these last days. This visitation will cause the end-time revival that has been spoken of by many seasoned saints of the Lord. Because of this fresh awakening of the Church, the message of the coming Kingdom of heaven will be proclaimed to a lost, dying, and desperate world in need of hope. Jesus declared, *"This gospel of the* [coming] *kingdom shall be preached…unto all nations; and then shall the end come"* (Matthew 24:14). Of course, the end-time Church cannot preach about the coming Kingdom and not include the coming *King* of the Kingdom. Christ is coming to establish His heavenly Kingdom. THIS

TRUTH IS OUR GREAT HOPE!

Earthly blessings are wonderful and enjoyable, but they pale in comparison to the divine HOPE that is set before us. This book is about this great heavenly HOPE and how we can lay hold of it.

PART 1

Hope, Essential for Wellness and Rest

*Now our Lord Jesus Christ himself, and God, even our Father, which hath loved us, and hath given us everlasting consolation and **good hope** through grace.*

— 2 Thessalonians 2:16

Chapter 1

Hope Versus Hopelessness

For the soul to find rest and a sense of well-being, it *must* have hope. When the soul is without hope, feelings of despair ensue. Isaiah 8:22 provides a perfect example of this fact. The prophet Isaiah describes the state of ensuing despair: *"They shall look unto the earth; and behold trouble and darkness, dimness* [or gloom] *of anguish; and they shall be driven to darkness."* Where did they *"look"*? They looked at the earth, which can be a bad place to look. What did they *"behold"*? They beheld trouble, darkness, and the gloom of anguish. What happened when they did that? They were *"driven"* to a sense of hopelessness, a place of utter *"darkness."* We can easily fall into that same state today if we look around the earth, beholding its troubles and conflicts, both domestic and abroad.

When we are in a hopeless state, we tend to spiral downward. That downward spiral begins because of what we are looking upon. We can look at the earth today and lose hope. Unfortunately, things are going to get much worse. Troubles, anguish, gloom and despair are going to increase more and more. The people of Isaiah's time looked upon the earth and *saw*. What they saw caused them to be *"driven to darkness."* That is, they were driven, further and further, into a pit of dark depression.

Two verses down, Isaiah (9:2) continues with this: *"people that walked in darkness."* These people (who had lived in a state of hopelessness) *"have **seen** a great light."* That light is the light of hope. *"They that dwell in the land of the shadow of death* [who dwelt in a place of perpetual doom and gloom], *upon them hath the light shined."* A shining light in a deep pit of darkness brings about great hope. Verse 3 says the shining light *"multiplied the nation, and... increased the joy: they joy before **thee**."*

The light they *saw* is the light of the Lord. When they saw this light, they rejoiced. Instead of doom and gloom, increase occurred. The nation was multiplied and joy increased. They rejoiced *before* the Lord, meaning He showed up in the midst of their despair. His light, which they set their eyes upon, dispelled the darkness. The Church, many years ago, sang of this triumph of light over darkness. They sang:

> *I saw the light, I saw the light*
> *No more darkness, No more night*
> *Now I am happy, Now I am free*
> *Praise the Lord I saw the light*

Thank God, we can all see the light!

Focus on the Light

What caused them to go from doom, gloom, and despair to this upward spiral of increase and joy? Let's look at verse 2 again: *"The people that walked in darkness have **seen** a great light."* They had been looking at the trouble upon earth, but notice their focus now

14

shifted (from their troubles and desperate circumstances) to the light from heaven. And by shifting their focus, they shifted their state to one of well-being. What we choose to gaze upon will always affect our well-being, even from gloom to joy!

We have got to be careful about what we set our focus (or gaze) upon. We must learn to take our eyes off of our circumstances and *see* the light. When the people of Isaiah's time set their gaze upon the light, which represented hope, it pulled them out of their state of gloom and anguish, taking them over into joy. The light they gazed upon was the light of the Lord. When the Lord showed up and they stood before Him, all despondency fled. That's a wonderful reality. We must position and train ourselves to live this way, especially in the days ahead. We must regularly stand before the Lord that we might gaze upon Him. If we do, we will never spiral down into an emotional pit of despair. It's a guarantee! *"In thy presence is fullness of joy"* (Psalm 16:11). When the issues of life distract our focus from the Lord, we begin to spiral down into a pit. Jesus promised, *"I am the light of the world: he that followeth me shall not walk in darkness, but shall have the light of life"* (John 8:12). Jesus does not lie. What he says is true!

If we focus on the earth, we are going to be very discouraged. The world (and our own country) is on this downward spiral. But we do not have to go down with it! Jobs are going to become scarce. According to many experts, the economy is going to plummet like you've never seen or imagined. It's coming. If we set our gaze upon that, we are going to experience great troubles. However, the light of the Lord is the light of hope. Those living in darkness, anguish, and despair have need of *hope*. They need, first and foremost, a vision of a prosperous, stable future.

Again, Jesus is *"the **light** of the world"* (John 8:12). When

Israel saw the light, they saw Jesus; they saw the Lord. The Word also tells us that Jesus *is* our hope. Paul said it this way: "*Lord Jesus Christ, which is **our hope**"* (1 Timothy 1:1). Because Jesus Christ is first and foremost our hope, it automatically makes Him our peace and joy as well. Hopeless people are joyless people, and their souls are restless.

We can't separate light from hope—Jesus is equally both. Jesus' light is our **hope.** The Bible never says Jesus is our *faith,* but it does say Jesus is our *hope.* Jesus *is* the *author* of our faith (Hebrews 12:2), but He *is* our hope.

When hope comes, anguish of soul ceases. Let me repeat that because we are going to need this in our future: When the light of heaven shines on the soul, the anguish of soul is over. Hopelessness is a place of great darkness of the soul. When the light comes, hopelessness dissipates. We saw this in Scripture from Isaiah. Israel was greatly despondent until the light came. It is the same for us today. The light of hope drives away all darkness.

> *"The light shines on in the darkness, for the darkness has never overpowered it."* (John 1:5, AMP)

In the next chapter, I share a personal experience, which took me from hell's hopelessness to heaven's great hope.

Chapter 2

Hell's Hopelessness to Heaven's Great Hope

I once found myself in a pit of despair, great dejection, and gloomy darkness. It had a firm grip on my soul. But in my anguish of soul, the Light appeared. And in the presence of the Lord, my night turned into day. Because when He shows up, things change. Hallelujah!

I'm ashamed to say this, but in my state of anguish, I hit a door with my fist, wishing I could hit God. Now that's a terrible thing. When your sorrow is so acute that you make a fist and hit a door wishing it was the face of God, you're in trouble! Perhaps you've never been there yourself, but you may experience something like this one day. Anguish and despair can be horrible.

Isaiah 8:21 says, "*They shall fret themselves.*" According to Strong's Concordance the Hebrew word translated "fret" means *to burst out in rage and anger*. Well, that's where I was because of my despair and anguish. I burst out in an angry rage against God. Let's read on in this verse: "*They shall fret themselves and curse their king and their God and look upward.*" Notice that in Israel's despair, they looked up and cursed their God. These are the people of God—Israel!

That *was* Victor Morgan. I burst out in such a fit of anger that I didn't look up to God to bless Him. Instead, I looked up to God to curse Him. Today, I'm ashamed to tell you this, but I tell you with the hope that it will help someone reading this. I lived through this and I understand it. We just read where the people of God, in their despair, looked up to heaven and cursed God. (Hopelessness is terrible beyond description. It really is.) When I hit the door in great anger, He, with abundant love, spoke to me. This is so amazing! God loves us so tenderly, *despite* our anger or despair, even when our anger is directed toward Him.

For example, at Calvary, Jesus was cruelly mistreated—beaten, spat on, and stripped naked. He was then nailed to a cross. Yet, the love of the Lord was so strong (in the midst of His accusers' hostile anger) that He forgave them without them ever asking. He said, "*Father, forgive them; for they know not what they do*" (Luke 23:34). I have experienced that side of the Lord. When you are so mad that you want to fight Him, He just pats you on the head and says, "I love you."

Understanding and Love

When I hit that door, wanting to hit God, He spoke to me with a heart of abundant love. This is exactly what He said—I add not one word, and I take not one word away—I repeat verbatim what He said to me: "*Victor I understand you, and because I understand you, I love you.*" That blew me away! At that point, I didn't even understand my own self. I was trying to fight God! In that moment of my greatest despair, He spoke that one sentence to me, and it was clear. He always calls me by my first name. Jesus is very personable.

He understood my depression. He loved me in spite of it and through it—and even out of it!

Paul had a similar experience with the Lord. In Scripture we see how hostile he was against the Lord. Yet, the Lord Jesus lovingly appeared to Paul and said, *"Saul, Saul* [who is Paul] *why persecutest thou me?"* (Acts 9:4). Later Paul wrote about this encounter and said he *"was before a blasphemer, and a persecutor, and injurious; but I obtained mercy, because I did it ignorantly in unbelief. And the grace of the Lord was exceedingly abundant with faith and love which is in Christ Jesus"* (I Timothy 1:13-14). I have learned first-hand, that when we ignorantly misdirect our anger towards the Lord, He does not respond in turn with anger. He always responds in love!

When Jesus said to me, "Victor, I understand you, and because I understand you I love you," it was remarkable to me. I had never heard this statement, before or after. In it was a great revelation—**the Lord's ability to love us is based on His ability to understand us.** And I have learned since, there are many Bible verses that bring this truth out. We will read a few as we proceed.

This truth, which the Lord revealed to me about Himself, can help us in our own relationships. The more we seek to understand others, the greater capacity we will have to love them. If we know why someone has kicked a door in rage, we can love them in spite of this. If we don't understand why they act that way, it's hard to love them in their misbehavior. Jesus' heart is full of loving compassion toward *all* men, because He understands *all* men.

The Lord delivered me from a state of despair by revealing His love for me. He showed me what His love for me is truly based upon.

Whatever you are dealing with that is so overwhelming, causing you to sink into defeat, the Lord *understands*. He knows your situation far better than you do. Therefore, He can *love* you in the midst of your feelings of defeat and shame. Because He understands *why* you're there and *how* you got there, even when *you* don't fully get it. He can love you in spite of your current state. The Lord understands that which we may not ever comprehend. Jesus sees the whole picture, while we only see and know in part (1 Corinthians 13:12). Even ourselves, we only know and understand in part.

For instance, He understood when my mother rejected me, even while I was in her womb. He knew the effect that would have upon me, better than I could have ever known. My mother had two children as a teenager. She felt as though she had been robbed of a lot by the time I came along. She just didn't want another child. Her attitude negatively affected me. Such things as negative attitudes, poor diet, anxiety, pesticides on food, and other innumerable variables can affect the state of the fetus while still in a mother's womb. Jesus fully understands *all* these factors.

It is worth noting that during my bout of anger against God, I had already been saved, Spirit-filled, and was in ministry. Yet, I wanted to fight God. I loved Him with all my heart, but I was carrying many issues. I was in a state of dejection. Satan had subtly distracted me, so as to shift my focus away from the Lord and onto myself. When I lost focus of Him, I lost my joy. Indeed, seeing only my frailties was quite depressing. When the great prophet Elijah was distracted from the Lord and focused only on his own frailties, he cried in despair: "*O LORD, take away my life; for I am not better than my fathers*" (1 Kings 19:4). Moses also had a similar experience with the *spirit of darkness*, and he too cried in his despair: "*Kill me, I pray thee…and let me not see my wretchedness*" (Numbers 11:15). Both of these great men of God spoke to Him from an acute awareness of their own frailties apart from God, and was consequently, absolutely disgusted with themselves.

The Lord delivered me from my own despair by revealing His constant love for me, based upon His perfect understanding of me. He deposited hope into my heart, so that, I would never be ashamed or feel shameful disgrace ever again. We see in Scripture that when Israel saw the light, hope sprang in them, and their situation changed.

Because of God's love for me, I am convinced that my future will always be bright. Knowing His great love for me, gives me great hope. I don't have days of hopeless despair as I once did anymore. Christians who live, day by day, with crippling despair have not understood God's great love for them. He understands everything His children go through. If you can receive that, you will be inspired to hope. Can you receive that today? If so, you will be inspired to hope. And when you have hope, you have well-being and a soul at rest. (I will expound much more about this concept further along in the book.)

When we have hope, we no longer have episodes of disgraceful shame again. Romans 5:5 says, "***Hope*** *maketh not ashamed.*" But what is this hope based upon? Let us keep reading: "*Because the **love of God** is shed abroad in our hearts by the Holy Ghost.*" Notice, it is because of *the love of God* that we have hope. And when we have Holy Spirit inspired hope, we never have to carry disparaging shame in our lives. We have a life of restful peace. Never do we struggle again with disgraceful, shameful troubles of soul, because hope lifts us up above it all. Jesus said to everyone who was heavy laden of soul *"come to me…and you shall find rest unto your soul"* (Matthew 11:28, 29). Hope lifts us up from our struggle. However, hope is predicated on our understanding of God's love for us. For me, this is not just a doctrine. This verse is an experience I've lived through!

God's Gift of Hope

God is our loving, heavenly Father, and He is *absolutely* good. 2 Thessalonians 2:16, says, *"Now **our** Lord Jesus Christ himself, and God, even **our** Father which hath **loved us**, and **hath given** us everlasting consolation* [encouragement] *and **good hope** through grace."* Thank God, Jesus is ours—He belongs to us! When you love somebody, you give to them. God loves us, and He has given us *"good **hope** through grace"* as a gift of His love! Whatever God gives us through grace is a *gift, b*ecause *grace* means we didn't earn it. The Greek word translated "grace" in this Scripture is translated "gift" in other verses. Whatever God gives us through *grace* is a *gift* to us. What God wants to give us as a gift is *"good hope."* He gave me hope as a gift, and I remember the moment I received it. This verse says that Jesus Christ and God, the Father, because of their love for us, have given us hope. It's a gift of love!

Let us read on to verse 17: *"**Comfort** your hearts, and **stablish** you in every good word and work."* He gives us this hope so that we can have comfort in our hearts. These aren't just words on a page to me. I'm truly reading my own experience. This good hope, through grace, is to *comfort* our hearts and *establish* us. Since that day, when God spoke to me, I have been established. It was not until He gave me this hope, that I found stability in life. There is an amazing power in hope. Hope is so precious. He gives us this as a gift because of His love for us. Therefore, we can be established no matter our circumstances. We can feel comfort. Hope gives us a state of well-being.

He wants to *"stablish you in every good word and work."* What does this mean? When you are full of His *good hope*, you are encouraged to do what's right in His sight. You aren't defeated; you aren't cursing God; you're not hitting doors, as I did. When you have *good hope*, you aren't acting out or speaking out in rage. Hope causes us to live well. It causes us to be filled with *"every good word and work."* We don't despair before God anymore when, through His love, He gives us good hope.

Infinite and Everlasting

*"His understanding is **infinite**"* (Psalm 147:5). Because of this fact, His love is also infinite. The gracious Lord revealed to me that His love is based upon His understanding. Hence, the Lord declares, *"I have loved thee with an **everlasting** love"* (Jeremiah 31:3). Again, the Lord loves us to the degree of His ability to understand us. He does not love beyond His understanding. He loves *because* of His understanding. Thank God, His understanding is *"infinite,"* and therefore, His love is *"everlasting."* The Lord revealed to me that He loves every human being everlastingly, because He ALONE understands every human being infinitely. I never knew that the love of God had a foundation until He told me. The foundation of God's love for humanity is in His ability to understand all humanity. We can say that God's love is founded upon understanding. This is why we are told in Scripture to *"get understanding"* (Proverbs 4:5, 7). Without it, we cannot really love—at least not as God does.

God understood what Israel needed when they were in such despondency. The Bible says they looked up and cursed God. But God understood that what they needed was the gift of hope. And so, He caused them to see the light of His hope. Instantly, their cursing changed into rejoicing!

I understand this, because it also happened to me. My anger changed into gleeful joy. Hallelujah! It was a supernatural thing; it wasn't natural. I wanted to fight the God who made me. And He lovingly said, "Victor, I understand you." There was such tenderness and confident assurance in His voice, I could not doubt. I thought I knew He loved me, but I discovered I really didn't know the extent of His love until I heard Him speak to me: "Victor, I understand you, and because I understand you, I love you." This one statement from Christ changed my life forever. In this one sentence, He was saying to me, "Relax, take it easy, all is well. I am for you—no matter what. Nothing can ever make Me forsake you; nothing you think, do, or feel. I am with you to the end." See, because of the Lord's infinite understanding of me, He can love me in a way I could never fully understand or ever love myself. Isn't God absolutely wonderful? He's undeniably marvelous!

Chapter 3

Vexation of Hopelessness

A life of hopelessness is a life of emptiness—a life of anguish and despair. Without hope, the soul wanders, seeking a place of security, stability, and meaning. Hopelessness causes a longing in the soul. When people are without hope, they know there is something missing—something they are grasping for. Hopelessness creates a hole in the soul, which the soul then seeks to fill, often in improper ways. People who are hopeless do many things to try and fill what they sense is missing.

A person without hope has no spark, no vitality, and no strength to endure. However, hope is always positive of the future. It provides a good outlook for today and is always optimistic about tomorrow. No matter how it looks at the moment, things will be all right. It, therefore, gives us a sense of well-being, even for today. This is the power of hope. As the Bible says, it will *"comfort your hearts"* (2 Thessalonians 2:17). It doesn't say it will change your circumstances. It says that it comforts your heart. A person with no hope for the future will act in desperate ways, seeking a better tomorrow. But such people make their tomorrows worse, because they seek security in wrong places, and in wrong ways.

Foolish Choices

In Ezekiel 19:1, we find the Lord speaking to and through the prophet: "*Moreover take thou up a **lamentation** for the **princes** of Israel.*" Princes are the sons of kings, and thus potential kings. This prophecy was to the potential kings of Israel. Why would God tell the prophet to lament a potential king? Let us keep reading, "*Moreover take thou up a lamentation for the princes of Israel. And say, What is thy mother? A lioness.*" Verse 5: "*Now when she* [Israel] *saw that she had waited, and her **hope** was lost, then she took another of her whelps* [cubs], *and made him a young lion.*" A young lion is at the peak of his strength, ruling his territory as king. But when Israel put a cub in the place of a young lion, it was not yet experienced, nor had it developed adequately to rule as king. A whelp (cub) could not fulfill the role of a young lion, for obvious reasons.

These verses speak of Israel's woes because of her choice of potential kings. When Israel lost her hope, in her desperation, she grabbed unqualified kings and put them into office. When Israel's "*hope was lost,*" she grasped one of her immature, untested cubs and made him a young lion. She put him in a place of strength. However, he was only an inexperienced cub. When people lose hope, they tend to do irrational things. Israel latched on to a person who was clearly ill-equipped to help them. People who lose hope lose their ability to exercise sound judgment.

America, too, has done what Israel did. When the economy failed in 2008, just before the presidential election of that year, many people were in despair and despondency. Many were fretting and frustrated—losing hope. So what did we do? We grabbed someone totally inexperienced, untried, and untested. When we are without hope, we make hasty decisions, because we feel a strong sense of desperation. Hopelessness creates a sense of franticness. When Americans thought: "We're losing hope, our future is ruined, the global economy has crashed," we grabbed someone inexperienced and put him over us. We took a cub and made him our king! The person we selected had **NO** executive experience prior to becoming president. He had only served eighteen months as a junior senator. He was behind in the polls until the financial bubble burst. Immediately, after the despair and bewilderment from that great tragedy, we elected to place Mr. Obama over us.

(At the time of this writing, we have not yet seen the full impact of the consequences from our hasty choice. Actually, the whole world seemed to have been in agreement with our choice, as the economic despair was felt globally. Now, the world is beginning to feel the effects of the choice we made for president—the one they too strongly supported. President Obama was given the Nobel Peace Prize shortly after his first inauguration "for the things *he was going to do* for world peace," the officiator said. Well, the world is now involved in more wars and upheaval of all kinds, largely due to President Obama's domestic and global policies. As Israel discovered, we, too, are now discovering: It's never a good idea to select a junior to do the job designed for the maturity of a senior. The world is in need of statesmen fathers.)

Let's take a closer look at what happened to Israel because of their hasty choice of a king. Verses 6 and 7 tell us, because of this young king's inexperience, he made a lot of rash decisions which hurt the people. Then verse 8 says, *"The nations set against him on every side from the provinces, and spread their net over him: he was taken in their pit."* This is why the prophet was told to lament the princes. Because Israel was going to make them kings and set them up to fail by putting them in positions of power before their time. It is an interesting point to note: God does not blame the rookie king; He says mourn for him. Rather, God blamed His people for losing their hope, and, thereby, irrationally choosing such a king.

Verse 9 tells us: *"And they put him in ward [a cage] in chains, and brought him to the king of Babylon."* Babylon caught the young king of Israel, put him in chains, put him in a cage, and took him to Babylon. Why did they do that? Because the enemies of Israel saw they had somebody in charge of Israel who had no experience — someone who didn't know what he was doing. This invited Israel's enemy to come in and attack. This only happened because Israel was in a state of hopelessness: *"Her hope was lost."*

Some young women and men make this mistake of acting in haste. If they are not married by a certain age, they begin to *feel* a sense of desperation, and out of that *feeling* they make bad choices, which they later regret. After the *spirit* of hopelessness has opened the door of their hearts, the *spirit* of desperation comes in. The spirit of desperation brings in, with itself, a spirit of insecurity and compromise. Our first mother, Eve, was plagued by these spirits of Satan, and in her despair, she made a tragic choice. Therefore, we must let God be our great hope, thereby, living with rest of soul (which is very attractive, indeed).

When we are in a state of hopelessness, we make irrational choices, which then intensify our despair. Consequently, everything we do and the things we pursue to make our lives better, only make them worse. Why does this happen? It is because we are without hope. Hope is invaluable for well-being and for a rested soul, out of which sound decisions are made.

We are going to have another round of bad times coming through in the not too distant future. As a result, we are going to see hopeless people making hasty, foolish choices. We *are* going to *see* it (just make sure it's not you). When people have a sense of hopelessness (individually or collectively), they drift over into despair. Languishing in despair, they make hasty decisions that make no sense. They experience a real sense of desperation. On the other hand, those who have what the Bible calls "*good hope*," have a comfort in their hearts no matter what—they are stable and established.

The Bible predicted (accurately, may I add) that in the last days, "cubs" would be leading the people: "*It shall come to pass in the last days…babes shall rule over them….Woe unto their soul!*" (Isaiah 2:2; 3:4, 9). What we are living through are the signs of the times. And there is much more to come. God's Word is amazingly exact. What it has spoken concerning the last days is happening and will continue to happen with great precision. Jesus said, "*This* [end time] *generation shall not pass away, till all be fulfilled*" (Luke 21:32). This is why, now more than ever, God wants to give His people GOOD HOPE.

Chasing Vanities

In Jeremiah 18:11 God tells the prophet: "*Speak to the **men of Judah**, and to the inhabitants of Jerusalem.*" These were God's people. Verse 12 says: "*And they* [the people of God] *said, **There is no hope**.*" In their state of hopelessness, they said, "*We will walk after our own devices, and we will every one do the imagination of his **evil** heart.*"

When we are hopeless, we do what's evil. We walk in the

imaginations of our own vanities. God tried to speak to Judah but they said, "It's hopeless; we've just lost hope. Even though we are the people of God, we've decided we want to walk in our own devices. We've decided we are going to do whatever evil we can imagine. Because we've given up hope in God, we've given up hope in eternal life, so why not live like heathens?" Hopeless people perpetually go down. The Word says when Israel was hopeless, they would be *"driven"* into darkness. A spark of hope can change all of that. In my deepest despondency and despair, the Lord spoke a sentence to me that gave me hope. I have lived out of that divine hope from then until now. And it has been glorious!

In Jeremiah 2:25, God is talking to Israel: *"Withhold thy foot from being unshod."* In other words, don't run so hard that you wear out your shoes; don't run out of your shoes and keep on going barefoot. God says, *"Withhold thy foot from being unshod* [without shoes], *and thy throat from thirst."* Don't run so hard that you dry your throat; don't run so hard that you are out of breath.

Why was Israel running so hard? Why were God's people expending so much energy in futility? Their throats had become dry and their shoes were worn out from chasing vanities. God said, *don't do it.* But they said, ***"There is no hope****: no; for I have loved strangers, and after them will I go." Strangers* represent the world and the ways of the world. Israel was saying, "We're going to run hard, we're running out of our shoes, and we're running out of breath. We're running hard out into the world, because we have lost our hope."

When I was in that state, I don't know what would have become of me if God hadn't shown up during my lowest moment. It's a frightening thought. Anytime you want to fight God, you've just about given up. Israel decided they would wear themselves out chasing the vanities of the world (even though they are God's people) because they had no hope. Depression can come upon the saved or unsaved. The reality is, a person full of good hope can never be depressed. If Satan can steal our hope, he can then chain us with depression.

Satan wants our hope because hope gives us a rested soul. Hope gives us stability in life, a sense of well-being. With hope, we won't run ourselves into the ground, chasing something that isn't even real. People with hope don't chase every Tom, Dick, and Harry (or Sue, Jane, and Mary). They don't run themselves ragged because they need something or someone to feel secure. They know, "I'm okay. My heart is at peace because of God's hope in me."

No Hope, No Life

In Ezekiel 37:11, God speaks to His prophet concerning Israel. He says, "*Son of man, these bones are the whole house of Israel.*" The whole house of Israel is nothing but bones! "*These bones are the **whole** house of Israel: behold, they say, our bones are dried, and **our hope is lost**.*" When we are without hope, our lives are full of dryness and death. Why was Israel so dead and dry? Why were they just bones without any skin? Because they declared, "*Our **hope** is lost.*"

God says, "*Therefore give them a word from Me.*" Do you know why God wanted Ezekiel to give Israel a word when they had no hope? It's because a word from God inspires hope. When they said, "*There is no hope,*" God said give them a word. True hope is based upon a true word from the Lord. In my experience, the Lord gave me a prophetic word, that brought me from a dead, dry place, to a place of life and joy!

When, like them, I felt as dry as dry bones and there was no

31

spiritual light, He gave me a word. And He has a word for you!

> *Therefore prophesy and say unto them, thus saith the Lord GOD; Behold, O my people, I will open your graves, and cause you to come up out of your graves, and bring you into the land of Israel (v. 12).*

What was He giving them? He was giving them something to hope for. He didn't say, "Maybe I will." He said, "*I will.*" God spoke to them about their future. He gave them something positive to look forward to—something to pick them up out of their despair—something to lift them out of their hopelessness. A person without hope is like the walking dead. It is so important that we receive from God this wonderful gift of hope, given from a loving Father to His precious children. It is called "**GOOD HOPE.**"

> *Lord, give us this glorious hope. We need a divine vision of our future. Give us this good hope. Grant us this precious gift from Your hand. We reach up, and we take it, O God. Thank You for releasing it to us. Hallelujah! Amen.*

No Strength

Let's look at Lamentations 3:18. The prophet Jeremiah is speaking of himself: "***My strength*** *and* ***my hope is perished.***" Notice, when we are without hope, we are without strength of soul. We cannot have strength and endurance if we are hopeless. This great devoted man of God had lost his hope in God.

Then the next word Jeremiah says is *remembering*. The

"ing" means it is in a constant present state: remember*ing*. Why was Jeremiah hopeless? Let's see what he was in the process of remembering: *"Remembering **mine** affliction and **my** misery"* (*v.* 19). Well, if you set your face upon *you*, of course you are going to fall down. *"Remembering mine affliction and my misery, the wormwood* [bitterness] *and the gall* [poison]." He said, "Remembering my state of bitterness; remembering my life of poison; when I was remembering these things, I had lost all hope, I had no strength, and I had no inspiration."

The Lord's Mercies

As we read on in Lamentations 3:21, Jeremiah said, *"This I recall to my mind, therefore **have I hope**."* When he was in the former state of mind, he didn't have hope, but now he's recalling something which gives him hope. What did he recall that took him from a state of hopelessness to a state of hope? He recalled: *"It is of the LORD's mercies that we are not consumed"* (*v.* 22). Jeremiah took his focus off himself and back over to the Lord, where it belonged.

Jeremiah said, "I'm going through hell, but, wait a minute, I'm still standing. I'm going through pain, but I'm still breathing. I remember that I'm not dead." And that began to offer him hope. *"This I recall to my mind, therefore have **I hope**. It is of **the LORD's mercies** that we are not consumed, because **his compassions** fail not. They are new every morning: great is **thy faithfulness**"* (*vv.* 21-23). When Jeremiah had focused on himself, he had no hope. Hope came when he began to focus on God. Hallelujah!

Do you know why I had been so dejected and angry at God? It was because I was focused on *me*, and blamed Him for my plight. But then God helped me to see *Him*. He said, *"I understand you, and because I understand you, I love you.*" That was His way of saying, "*I'm merciful, I'm faithful, and every morning I'm with you.*" Glory! I never felt alone again. The days of utter despair were over!

The state of Jeremiah's mind was the determining factor as to whether or not he would have hope. Jeremiah continued in verse 24: "*The LORD is my portion, saith my soul.*" When he remembered God, then he made a confession of his faith: "*The LORD is my portion, saith my soul; therefore will I **hope** in him.*" Do you see this? He had lost hope in God, but when he started thinking about the goodness and faithfulness of His God, hope revived in him. And his renewed hope gave him a positive outlook on life.

Why had Jeremiah lost hope in God? He had said, "*My strength and my **hope** are perished.*" Without hope there is no will to continue. He said, "I don't have any strength." Hopelessness is why some people die. And hope is the reason why people, who should have died, keep living. It is hope that keeps them going. Jeremiah had focused on his negative state. He, therefore, felt overwhelmed. In hopelessness, he confessed, "My life is over."

Then he began remembering the attributes of God and the truth of God. This caused him to hope once again. As a result, instead of negative confessions, he began to have faith-filled confessions. He put his hope in God. Hopelessness drags us down, but meditating on and speaking God's truth brings hope, which lifts us up. It does not change the circumstances, but it lifts us above them in our hearts and minds.

Chapter 4

Blessedness of Hope

We find, through Scripture and other examples as well, that it is what we focus on that causes us to be either hopeless or hopeful. When we look up, we receive hope. And there are many rewards that result from that upward gaze.

Rest and Strength

In Acts 2:25-26, the apostle Peter is preaching his first sermon after Jesus' resurrection. Listen to what he said: "*For David speaketh concerning him* [Jesus], *I foresaw the Lord **always** before my face… **therefore** did my heart rejoice, and my tongue was glad; moreover also my flesh shall **rest in hope**.*" If we keep our eyes upward toward heaven, we will always have hope; just as Jesus did—*no matter* the circumstance. Jesus is our example in all things. And He shows us the secret of a restful soul. It is hope received through "*always*" looking upward. In the midst of Jesus' most horrible trial—His crucifixion—He looked up to the Father and thereby His soul rested in hope, which manifested in joy.

Jesus experienced many negative circumstances. These could

have gotten Him down every day, but He kept His face toward God. And in keeping His face toward God, He always had hope. His hope gave Him stability of soul. Again, hope provides a sense of well-being. Hope is an essential gift from the Father, given for the well-being of His precious children.

Joel 3.16 says, *"The LORD will be the **hope** of his people."* It doesn't say the Lord will be the faith of His people. God is not our faith; He *gives* us faith. The Lord is the *author* of our faith, but He's not faith itself. However, many times the Bible says He *is* hope. So, when the Lord gives us hope, He is really giving us more of Himself (or showing us more of Himself). *"The LORD will be **the hope** of his people, **and the strength** of the children of Israel."* When we have hope, we have strength. As we have seen, when Jeremiah had lost hope, he said he didn't have any strength. Yet when the soul of a man is encouraged, he has strength to endure.

God wants to be our hope, so we, His children, can be strong. When God's people have hope, they also have strength. They endure all tests because they can see the end, and they know they win! Jesus had strength to carry on through His greatest trial, because He taught Himself to *"rest in **hope**"* by *"always"* looking up to see the face of the Father.

Good Outlook, Sense of Well-Being

One of our church members had previously developed cancer, and now, unfortunately, the cancer had returned. But when my wife and I went to visit her, she was just as happy as could be. She said, "I'm already healed. I know I am. I'm just walking it through." She was full of peace. It was amazing, astounding really, at her mature age. I said, "Well, praise God. You are just walking it through. You are just resting in God. You're refreshed and at ease, aren't you?" She was just as happy as one could be. You see that's what hope does. Hope says, "I know tomorrow is going to be fine, because I know the Lord loves me." It was not long before the Lord granted her a new clean bill of health. Hope opens up the way for a speedy recovery, whereas, a hopeless person lingers in darkness and even hastens death.

First Corinthians 13:7 says regarding *agape* love—or God's love—that it "***Hopeth*** *all things."* When we possess agape love, it produces this kind of hope. As we learned from Romans 5:5, "***Hope*** *maketh not ashamed; because* [of] *the love of God."* Agape love "***hopeth*** *all things."* No matter what's going on, through God's love, there is hope—hope in all things. When we have hope, through any situation, we can endure. When we have hope, we have the fortitude to overcome anything. We only feel overwhelmed, or want to quit, when we lose our hope. Hope can only be sure when we are convinced of God's loves for us. You know He is there to see you through any situation because His love *"never faileth"* (*v.* 8).

We are living in the last days. God says in Malachi 4:5-6, that in the last days He wants the hearts of the children to be turned to the Father. Do you know why? It's because in these last days, like never before, we need to know the Father's heart. We, His children, need to know how much He loves us. Because His love will create a hope in us that will keep us stable, as we go through these difficult times.

God said, in these last days, He wants the hearts of His children to be turned to Him (as their Father), that they may know His heart. That's a revelation. More than ever, God wants you to *know* Him as a loving Father. Through His great love, He wants to encourage us with an unshakable hope. He wants us to know Him like that, so we can find comfort of heart, no matter how bad times get.

First Corinthians chapter 13 teaches us that if we have **hope** in all things, we can endure all things (*v.* 7). Our ability to *endure* is based on our ability to have *hope*. And divine hope is grounded on divine love. Or we can say: *Enduring hope is founded upon enduring love.*

Because I am convinced of how much my Father in heaven loves me, I actually like myself. If He loves me that much, I must be something special. I didn't always think that way, certainly not when my life was full of despondency and misery. Much like the prophet Jeremiah had thought of himself, and thus, was despondent. But when I caught hold of hope—heaven's hope—I gained a good outlook and sense of well-being. My soul now has rest!

In Acts 26:6 Paul says, "*And now **I stand** and am judged for the **hope of the promise**.*" It's the Word of God, the promise of God, which gives us a foundation for hope. Paul was in prison at the time. He was in chains, and he had been beaten. Yet he said, "*I stand.*" In other words, I'm not sitting. I'm not wallowing. I'm not crying. "*Now **I stand** and am judged for the **hope** of the promise made of God, unto our fathers. Unto which promise* [of eternal life] *our twelve tribes, instantly serving God day and night **hope** to come*" (*vv.* 6-7). When we have the promise of eternal life, it gives us hope to serve God both day and night. Therefore, I'm not shaken, I'm not disturbed, I'm not cursing, and I'm not backsliding. I'm serving God because I have hope in a promise. And that's, of course, eternal life. Paul understood his future was beautiful beyond description. And this understanding kept him encouraged—never discouraged—irrespective of his circumstances.

Paul said, you have beaten me, you have imprisoned me, you have chained me, but you haven't shaken my hope. I'm still standing! Hope gives us the strength to continue, no matter what. Paul based his ability to continue upon a certain hope: "*Unto which promise our twelve tribes, instantly serving God day and night **hope** to come. For which **hope's** sake, king Agrippa, I am accused of the Jews.*" He was accused because of this hope. Is your hope in heaven so obvious that people can accuse you of it?

Going on with verse 8, we read: "*Why should it be thought a thing incredible with you, that God should raise the dead?*" Paul had hope in eternal life. He said, "My hope knows that, even if you guys cut my head off, I will rise again. I have a hope. I have a confident outlook. I'm positive that my future is secure. You don't faze me a bit, because I've got a great hope!"

This is what hope does for the soul. Do you now understand this wonderful hope? It is given to us as a gift. God has given us this good hope through grace.

The Helmet of Hope

I will close this chapter providing a glimpse into Paul's understanding of the purpose and place of hope in the believer's life.

In Paul's first letter to the Thessalonian church in chapter five, he said, concerning the last days with its sorrows and troubles: "*Sudden destruction cometh upon **them**" (v. 3)— "them*" or those who are not right with God. Then he said to the believer, in light of the approaching times of upheaval, to **be sober-minded** (v. 8). In other words, don't let the problems of this world cause you to become mentally unbalanced and fretful. But how can we be sober-minded in the midst of utter "*destruction*"? Paul goes on to tell believers to put on "*for a helmet the **hope** of salvation*" (v. 8). Paul understood that believers could protect their minds from the despair of the times by putting on HOPE as a helmet.

HOPE PROTECTS THE MIND IN TROUBLESOME TIMES!

Hope holds the mind stable through the storm, until a bright, sunny day dawns—the day of the Lord's glorious return.

Thank You for hope, Father. Thank You for this thing that gives Your people soundness of mind and a sense of well-being. When some are going to be killing themselves and others, getting intoxicated, or doing whatever evil their imaginations can come up with out of desperation, that won't be the case with us, Lord. It won't be so for the people of God! You give us something so incredible that our hearts always feel comforted. Hallelujah! Thank You for our hope. Help Your people to embrace it, Father. Help them to acknowledge it daily, especially as we have come to the end of time. Give us a revelation of the Father's love. Help us to know, like never before, that Your heart is truly toward us. Help us to see it, Father, and find comfort and peace in this reality. We thank You for this. We give You the praise. Amen.

PART II

"Look Up!" Heaven's Hope for Earth's Troubles

*But he being full of the Holy Ghost, **looked up** steadfastly **into heaven**, and saw the glory of God, and Jesus standing on the right hand of God.*

— Acts 7:55

Chapter 5

A World in Turmoil

God has commanded the end-time believer to *look up* in these last days of trouble. The Church must understand what's happening in the earth and why the saints of God must be regularly encouraged to look up in light of the times.

Wars

In Luke 21:9, Jesus answered the disciples' questions: When will the end be? What will be the signs of the end of time? How will we know when we are living at the end of the world, the end of this earth age? Jesus replied, *"Ye shall hear of wars…"* (That's one sign, and we hear that everywhere, don't we?) *"When ye shall hear of wars and commotions* [trouble everywhere]*, be not terrified."* Don't be terrified. Even though, the last days will, indeed, be terrifying. There will be terrors, specifically initiated to bring about emotional trauma in the hearts of people. But Jesus told His disciples, "When you hear of these commotions, don't *you* be terrified." *"But when ye shall hear of wars and commotions, be not terrified: for these things **must first** come to pass."* These things **must** happen. Jesus is telling us, "There are some things that have to happen **first**. Before I can get you out of here, some dreadful things must happen, and you must learn to live through them."

As believers, if we didn't have to go through anything during the end-times, Jesus would have never said that those who *endure* to the end shall be saved (Matthew 24:13). We have to be able to *endure* some things to make it through the days ahead. There will be trying times. Jesus said "*as a snare*" the trouble of the last days will "*come on all them that dwell on the face of the whole earth*" (Luke 21:35). Then He said to His followers: "*Watch ye **therefore**, and pray always*" (*v.* 36). These days will be like a "***snare.***" Jesus said, it shall come upon all of "***them.***" A snare is something that you do not see until it is too late, and it **catches you** off guard. Jesus said this is how it would be for *them*. But for *us* who believe, because we are *watching* and *praying*, Jesus said we can "***escape*** *all these things that shall come to pass*" (*v.* 36).

We are to "*pray always.*" Jesus said, as we persist in prayer, He will open our eyes to see the end-time *snares,* which will trap and enslave others. But we will be able to escape them. As we continue to pray, Jesus will open our eyes to see into the glory realm, that we may be encouraged, and thus, hope to the end for the coming glory of Christ. It is clear that Jesus wants His servants to escape the troubles of the end times, because He gave us the key to escape—persistent prayer!

Jesus said: "*These things must first come to pass*" (Luke 21:9). These things are not permanent. They **must first pass**! This will be the close of the earth as we now know it. Some things have to occur. But they are simply birth pangs, which will get us through to the other side. "*These things must first come to pass; but the end is not by and by* [or yet].*"* The end is not immediate. There will be a season of testing first.

I'm telling you, we are living in the end of days. Everything the Bible has spoken about, giving us the parameters to know when we are at the end of time, are already lining up. But notice, Jesus said you are going to see these things first, but it's not the end, it's not immediate. Certain traumatic events must first pass, and they will not be over in a day or two. Hence, we must *"endure unto the end."*

Earthquakes, Famines, Pestilences

Luke 21:10-11, tells us: *"Then said he unto them, Nation shall rise against nation, and kingdom against kingdom: And great earthquakes shall be in divers* [different] *places."* If you look up "earthquakes" in your computer's search engine, you will find that there have been more earthquakes than ever before, in various places around the globe. Jesus said we were going to see a lot of this in the last days. This is the time we are living in.

He says *"great earthquakes shall be in divers places, and famines* [due to drought and strange weather patterns], *and pestilences* [diseases, plagues]*; and fearful sights"* — and many other things that are just going to be blood curdling. It will be terrifying. But if we set our sights on these fearful signs of the end, we too will be frightened.

Hatred, Fear, and Perplexity

Luke 21:17 says, *"And ye* [My disciples] *shall be hated of all men."* If you're looking at what's going on today, even in America, Christianity is under great assault. Christians are being killed around the world, more than ever before. This type of violence had not occurred since the beginning of the Church (two thousand years ago). Christians are being killed, for the sake of Christ, more than ever before. Jesus said all this was going to happen. I'm telling you, the Church in America will not be exempt. It's coming our way. In fact, Christian oppression in America is already here. The spirit of antichrist is spreading. Because of that fact, it's almost dangerous to boldly stand up and confess our faith in Jesus Christ, even in some places in America.

Continuing in Luke, verse 25 tells us: *"there shall be signs in the sun, and in the moon, and in the stars; and upon the earth distress of nations* [globally]." We are living in that time now. Nations are feeling great distress *"with perplexity"*—with no way out. In these last days, the nations of the earth will experience *trouble* as never before, with *perplexity*—meaning, man will have no solution. They'll know no way out of it. Aren't we living in that time now?

The next verse, Luke 21:26, says, *"Men's hearts failing* **them**." Their hearts will fail *them*, Jesus said. But not *you*. Jesus separates the unsaved from the saved. Your heart should never fail you. You should never be terrorized or perplexed, nor should you walk in fear in these last days. This verse goes on to say, *"Men's hearts failing them for fear."* Jesus already told His disciples not to be fearful. The world today is full of fear, and it's going to intensify more and more. Increasingly, we are going to see hopeless people doing hideous things—murders and suicides. They're just going to give up. It's already happening, but it's going to get worse. The more unpleasantness in the world, the more God's people will have to *"look up"* beyond the mayhem and confusion upon the earth.

In Luke 21:26 Jesus continues, *"Men's hearts failing them for fear, and for* **looking after** *those things which are coming on the earth."* The Greek word translated "looking after" actually is more the idea of *looking ahead*. What are they going to be looking ahead to? To the things that are *coming*, and they know they have no answers, nor solutions. Anyone in tune with the times can see that war is coming. In fact, it is here. And no one seems to be able to put a stop to it.

We are headed for a total economic collapse, on a global level. In these last days, men will see it, but they won't be able to stop it. So, for that reason, they will live in fear and in anticipation of the troubles. Another thing coming is pestilence (diseases and plagues). Ebola came, and so will other plagues. Man will not be able to stop them. People are living in fear of many things. Jesus said these things will come upon the earth. Men will be able to see them coming, but they will have no solutions or ability to do anything about them.

I'm going to be bold and make this statement: This generation is going to likely see America in a very serious war. Radical Islam, and our other enemies, will strike the homeland. Homeland security will not be able to prevent this. I had a dream a while ago, and I've had dreams like this before. I saw great devastation. As I stood, I saw everything leveled. Then I lifted up my eyes a little bit, and I saw buildings that were still standing. I knew this was a major city in America, almost completely leveled. The Bible says men will see these things coming, but they will not be able to do anything about it. For this reason, their hearts will fail. They will be perplexed, with no answers—helpless.

Verses 25 and 26 of Luke tell us that men will be looking forward to, or at, the things that are coming. They are "*looking after those things which are coming on the earth.*" They are looking after, they are looking at, they are looking forward, and they are anticipating a lot of horrible things coming upon the earth. Then the end of verse 26 tells us "*the powers of heaven shall be shaken.*" That means everything that can be shaken will be shaken (Hebrews 12:27).

Let's keep reading, because there is a good word coming.

Look Up!

Let us continue to verse 28: "*And when these things begin to come to pass.*" Well, we are living in the times when they are beginning to come to pass. "*And when these things begin to come to pass, then look up.*" Here's what I want you to see. Notice when Jesus said in verse 26: "*them*" and "*they.*" He was talking about those in the world who have no eternal hope. When they *look at* the earth and what's happening on earth (looking on what they are anticipating), they will faint. Their hearts will just quit. But He says while *they* are looking at the earth, *we* are to "*look up*" (*v.* 28). Hallelujah!

Jesus wants us to look up because, otherwise, we will go insane, much like the rest of the people upon earth. I'm telling you, the Church is going to survive! All *they* (those outside of the Church) have is the earth to look at and man to look to for solutions. But *we* have something that is beyond the earth that we can focus upon. That's why we are to *look up*. Jesus was talking about looking up into glory—looking up into the heavenly realm. In these last days, when calamities of all sorts break loose, Jesus tells the Church to look up into the heavenly realm. There are going to be more and more wars. Nations will rise against nations. There will be severe earthquakes in many places. There will be a rise in terrorist attacks, even in America. Also, there is coming famines and global shortages, which will spark wars among the nations, because their survival will be threatened. There will also be pestilences, which are plagues (a plague is a contagious, epidemic and deadly disease). Jesus clearly predicted all these things would happen in these last days, and much more. However, He told us (His disciples) to set our gaze upon that place of eternal peace, joy, and rest. We are to feed our hearts from the place He resides. We are to look up and fix our gaze upon heavenly realities. As we look up to Heaven, we will pray to Heaven, and Heaven will strengthen our hearts, so that we will not faint, as others will.

Chapter 6

Heavenly Realities, Our Focus

Get your gaze up into the glory realm. That's the way you will remain sane. That's the way we will all survive and prevent a mental breakdown. That's the way we will escape being terrorized or full of fear—when we set our focus upon our eternal home. We are to look beyond. We are to look past the drama being played out on the earth. We are told by the Lord to gaze up into heaven. Hallelujah! Jesus said, *"That ye may be accounted worthy to escape all these things"* (Luke 21:36). The Church will escape the troubles of the times, because we are learning to look up into the heavenly realm.

Look at Luke, chapter 9:16: *"Then he* [Jesus] *took the five loaves and the two fishes, and **looking up** to heaven..."* What did He do? He did what He told us to do. He looked up! Where did He look up to? Heaven! That's what He means when He tells the Church, in the last days, *look up.* He's talking about looking up to the heavens, or heavenward. Jesus took His eyes off of the earth when there was a need the earth could not meet. He looked up to heaven, and so must we learn to do the same.

Focus on Our Eternal Home

Unprecedented calamities are going to break loose. The earth is going to reel and rock, and everything that can be shaken will be shaken (Hebrews 12:26–27). But you and I are to look up to heaven. O glory! We are to see heaven. We are to see the pearly gates. We are to see our eternal home. We are not to be moved or shaken. We believe in heaven! This earth is not our home.

Jesus practiced what He preached. I'm showing you what He told the Church to do in these dark days: *"Look up!"* Looking up to heaven takes your eyes off the earth and the economy. I know all of that is real. I watch it, but I don't stay fixed on it. I understand it all, but it only encourages me more and more to look up. The Savior is going to break the eastern sky (Matthew 24:27)!

In 2 Corinthians 4, the apostle Paul demonstrates how *we* are to look up. We know Paul went through a lot of troubles, trials, and tests. For his calling and his purpose, he suffered extensively. But because of his focus, he always had joy.

Paul said (in the present tense): *"We **are** troubled on every side, **yet not** distressed; we **are** perplexed, **but not** in despair"* (v. 8). He says, *"Yet not…but not."* *"We are troubled…we are perplexed,"* but we're not distressed or in despair. Paul had trouble on every side. In these last days, just ahead of us, there's going to be trouble on every side, too.

Notice what Paul did for the situation not to affect him. Look at verse 18: *"While we look **not** at the things which are seen."* As we gaze **not** upon the things that we are suffering upon the earth, we are free to look up to glory. That's why we are not perplexed like *they* are. That's why we don't become despondent like other people. Glory to God! *We* can look up, but *they* can't look up. They have no hope in the coming glory. Rather, their hope is in the White House (or government). But it will be silent. They have their hope in Wall Street, but it's going to collapse. They have their hope in their hospital insurance, but it's going to fail. Everything is going to be shaken. (Please read Isaiah 24:4-5, 19-21.)

Paul said we are not troubled in our hearts like other people *"while we look not at the things which are seen"* in the natural. We don't focus on that, *"but at the things which are not seen."* We focus on glory. We gaze upon heaven *"for the things which are seen are temporal; but the things which are not seen are eternal"* (2 Corinthians 4:18). In the midst of our earthly trouble, Paul was saying that we are to focus on heaven's eternity. We are to focus on the eternal realm of unspeakable grandeur and glory. Therefore, we will not be shaken, even though we are in the midst of trouble. We are never truly disturbed, even though we're living in perplexing times, because our focus is on the things above. If we don't focus on trouble, we can't feel troubled. If we focus on heavenly glory, we can only feel joy.

Paul was only doing what Jesus taught. In times of great trouble, he was looking up. You, too, are to lift your eyes up above earth. Lift your eyes up above what the world is going through. There will be much trouble, but that's fine with us, because we know our eternity is secure and that's what we are to be looking at. If a bomb goes off, fine. If we get a deadly disease, we won't fear. If we lose our house, fine. We have another mansion *"not made with hands, eternal in the heavens"* (2 Corinthians 5:1). In these times, these are the things we must focus on. Nothing here matters. *"Look up,"* Jesus said. Jesus lived by His own teaching, of course. Five times in the Bible it is recorded that Jesus *looked up,* always in reference to heaven. We will not be bothered like other people because we can look up. Hallelujah!

Joy Set Before Us

The Word says that in the last days, people will break down, and their hearts will fail (Luke 21:26). They will just give up and quit. They will live in a state of hopelessness. It's a terrible way to live, but the whole earth is headed there. However, the Church is going to be fine, if we can learn to look up. We have to practice it now. Learn to lift your eyes up and see the things that are eternal.

Hebrews 12:2 says: *"**Looking** unto Jesus."* Where is Jesus now? In Heaven! That's where we have to learn to look. Lift your eyes up. *"Looking unto Jesus the author and finisher of our faith; who for the **joy** that was set before him…"* That joy set before Him was heaven. Jesus said to His disciples on His way to the Cross, *"Rejoice, because I said, I go unto the Father"* (John 14:28).

We can't focus on heaven and be sad. We can't focus on eternal things and live in misery. The Bible says we live that way only when we set our gaze upon earth. I feel sorry for people in the Church who have no heavenly vision. They are going to be as hopeless as the man next door, who doesn't know God. The Bible says *"for the **joy** that was set before him."* He was able to despise the shame and endure the Cross, which was not a joyful thing. We know that it was the most hideous, horrible death known to man. Jesus set His gaze above earth and looked onto heaven. From that perspective, His heart was filled with joy—even as He was going to the Cross.

We must learn to follow Jesus' example. Now that He's in heaven, we have to focus our gaze upon Him. He is now seated at the right hand of God. In other words, *where He set His focus is where*

He ended up. Did He experience trouble? Was it unbearable (humanly speaking) and excruciatingly hard? Yes, what He went through was dreadful. It was hellish, but He set His gaze upon heaven.

Jesus, *"the author and finisher of our faith; who for the joy that was set before him endured the Cross"* and despised all the shame (Hebrews 12:2). He was hung naked, they plucked out His beard, and they spat on Him. It was shameful. But He went through it, because He focused on what brought Him joy. Jesus always focused on the things above.

I hope you are able to get this, for we have to be survivors of the coming catastrophes. We have to be able to make it through it okay, not falling apart or grumbling. We are to live a different way — with eternal hope.

In John 14:28, Jesus says, *"Ye have heard how I said unto you, I go away."* Heaven was His destination. He said, "You've heard, because I've told you several times, I'm going to heaven." Then He says, *"I go away, and come again unto you."* That's the rapture. He's coming back. He said, "I'm going to heaven, but I am coming back. I'm coming back at the end of time to get you out of the earth to be with Me in Heaven."

Then He said, *"If ye loved me, ye would **rejoice**, because I said, I go unto the Father."* You see, that was the joy that Jesus had set before Him. He went to the Father by way of the Cross. He went to the Father by way of suffering and disgrace. But He did not focus on the suffering or shame. He focused on **hope**. He said to His disciples, "If you can focus like Me, you will **rejoice** with Me." He didn't say, "I'm going to the Cross." He said, "I'm going to the Father." His focus was on the Father and on eternity. And when we focus on that, we, too, can rejoice no matter what.

Peace in Stormy Times

Jesus said in the prior verse (*v. 27*): "*Peace I leave with you, my peace I give unto you.*" He said, "I give you My peace, and I'm *leaving* My peace with you." Then He continued, "*Not as the world giveth, give I unto you. Let not your heart be troubled, neither let it be afraid.*" Jesus said that the unsaved people's hearts would fail them for fear. But He said to the disciples, and he's saying to us today, "Don't let that happen to you. You are going to see the powers of hell hang Me on a Cross. But I'm leaving for Heaven, and here is what your peace is based upon: the fact is I'm not only going, but I'm also coming back for you." Jesus told them, "*I go and prepare a place for you, I will come again, and receive you unto myself; that where I am, there ye may be also*" (*v. 3*).

Let this fact be your peace in the midst of stormy times — The Master is coming back. We are going to be okay. We have an eternal hope. We have to begin to focus on this in these days — on eternal reality, not on how to get to the "next level" here on earth, as many now seek. That is very shallow in light of eternity. Nobody's going to have a "next level" when tribulation breaks out. In light of the times, we have to focus on our eternal abode. It's far better to focus on getting to the *highest level* rather than earthly promotion. Jesus said, "*Strive to enter in* [Heaven]*.*" He said, "*Many I say unto you, will seek to enter in, and shall not be able*" (Luke 13:24). Let us devote our efforts to attaining this highest level, as opposed to some position here on earth. Paul, understanding this, said he forsook every great thing he had attained in this life, to "*press towards the mark for the prize of the **high calling** of God*" (Philippians 3:14). He said, "*Let us, therefore, as many as be perfect* [or mature]*, be thus minded.*" Then, he said he wept over Christians "*who mind earthly things*" (Philippians 3:15, 19). Let us all be concerned that we focus on the highest level and strive for that, and not be content with anything less.

Chapter 7

Gazing Upon Heavenly Realities

Jesus always looked forward to what was promised or what was His future. He didn't get bogged down by the terrible things that were happening to Him. He always had His gaze on the realities of heaven set before Him.

Have Joy and Rejoice

In John 14:30, Jesus said, *"Hereafter I will not talk much with you: for the prince of this world cometh."* This means, *Satan has one last, grand attack to plot My death and kill Me.* Yet in verse 28 He said, *"Rejoice because I'm going to the Father."* He said *"Rejoice,"* but He then said that Satan was coming. The prince of this world is Satan and he was coming to take Jesus' life.

Yet Satan, and his diabolical activities, were not what Jesus was focused on. He focused on heaven not on earth or Satan. The earth is Satan's domain. Jesus called him *"the prince of this world."* He focused on heavenly realities, not on earth's temporal things.

Jesus taught His disciples that they too, could always live in peace if they believed that He was not only going to Heaven, but also coming back for them.

In John 13, verse 27, Jesus says, *"And after the sop* [the Last Supper] *Satan entered into him* [Judas]. *Then said Jesus unto him, that thou doest, do quickly."* Jesus knew Satan had entered Judas and that His time on earth was just another day or two. But He still said, *"If ye loved me, ye would rejoice"* (14:28). Jesus knew He was about to experience untold suffering on the Cross, but that was not His focus. His focus was on the Father in Heaven. His eyes were fixed on His eternal hope.

It's time to focus on eternal realities, because our comfortable lives, in the natural, may not last too much longer. In John 14:1, Jesus said, *"Let not your heart be troubled."* There He goes again! He said men's hearts would fail *them* in these last days. But here He said don't let *your* hearts be troubled. He tells us, if *"ye believe in God, believe also in me."*

In verse 2 He said, *"In my Father's house are many mansions: if it were not so, I would have told you. I go to prepare a place for you."* He was saying, "Don't let your hearts be troubled. No matter what you go through on earth, if you *truly* believe in me, then believe this: I go to prepare a place for you that you may be with Me eternally." Don't you be troubled for anything! We have a place prepared and it's over in glory! It's in the eternal realm. It's in a place called Heaven. It's in the Father's house. You and I have mansions waiting for us. Why should we fall apart because of the light affliction here on earth? When you can set your hope in this, you'll not be troubled. You're troubled only when you believe in what you can see with your natural eyesight. But thank God that we live by faith, not by sight.

John 15:11, tells us: *"These things have I spoken unto you, that my joy might remain in you."* Jesus was saying: "I'm going to heaven, and I'm going to get you up there, too. I'm telling you these things so that you can have joy. On earth, you are going to have unrest. There is going to be a lot of trouble on earth. But be of good cheer, I have overcome the earth. I'm going to heaven. I'm breaking through earth's orbit. I've broken the gravity pull. I'm going to heaven. If you believe Me, you should have peace, because I told you I'm coming back for you; where I am, you shall be also. I'm telling you these things so that you can have joy." Hallelujah!

Now, if you don't hear these things, in light of what's coming, you are not going to have any joy. You will be depressed like your co-workers. But while they are full of confusion because there are no answers, you will yet be walking with a song on your lips. This is for the believing ones. Jesus said, *"These things have I spoken unto **you**, that **my** joy might remain in **you** and that **your** joy might be **full**"* (John 15:11).

Jesus said in John 14:1, If you *"believe in God, believe also in me."* He said, "I'm leaving; I'm going back to the Father. But I'm coming back for you. I'm going to prepare mansions for you." If we can set our hope in this, nothing on earth will disturb us. That's why Jesus says to the believer, "When all this tribulation breaks loose upon earth, lift up your eyes. Look up, look up, look up!" Let us focus on what Jesus is doing for us in Heaven, not on what Satan is doing on earth.

In Acts 2:23, Peter was talking about the crucifixion of Jesus: *"being delivered by the determinate counsel and foreknowledge of God, ye have taken, and by wicked hands have crucified and slain."* Verse 25: *"For David speaketh concerning him* [Jesus]*, I foresaw the Lord always before my face."* Notice here, in the context of the Cross,

Jesus kept the Lord before His face. That's why the Bible says *"for the joy that was set before him"* (Hebrews 12:2). Jesus was always looking up, not at what was happening on earth.

Because Jesus kept His Father before His face, Acts 2:26 says, *"Therefore did my heart rejoice."* In the midst of the Cross, His joy was in seeing the Father. They tied Him up, they whipped Him, they dragged Him from judgment hall to judgment hall, but the Bible says that He didn't say a word. Do you know why? His gaze was upon the Father. He had joy in His heart, because He thought, "I'm coming; I'm coming, Father; I'm coming to join You in heaven— full of glory, full of magnificence!" That's why He told Judas concerning his betrayal, *"That thou doest, do quickly"* (John 13:27). Jesus was anxious to go home and be with the Father.

> *I can't wait for it to happen! I'm going to heaven! Jesus, if it takes all this trouble to redeem my soul out of this earth, my God, do it quickly. Let the economy fall quickly. Let the wars happen quickly. Let disease break out quickly. Let's just get it over with. Glory to God!*

(Remember, Jesus did say these things **must** happen to usher in His return for us. He said, *"All these are the **beginning** of sorrows"* (Matthew 27:8). Meaning that at the end of time it would be like a woman in labor—the pains come quicker and quicker, and they are more and more intense. But He also said, *"A woman, when she is in travail* [giving birth], *hath sorrow, because her hour is come, but as soon as she is delivered of the child, she remembereth no more the anguish, for joy that a man is born into the world"* (John 16:21). This same wonderful truth is seen in Revelation by John. When John was caught up to Heaven he said, *"I beheld and, lo* [behold] *a great* *multitude, which no man could number, of all nations, and kindreds, and people, and tongues, stood before the throne* [in Heaven]…*These are they who came out of great tribulation* [or the birth pangs of the last days]…*and God shall wipe away all tears from their eyes*" (Revelation 7:9, 14, 17). Point being: If we must go through pain **here**, to enter into the everlasting joy of the Lord **there**, so be it. Amen.)

Now back to Acts chapter two. Let's look at verse 32: "*This Jesus hath God raised up.*" God raised Him up, and Jesus is seated at the right hand of God the Father (Mark 16:19). This place of glory and splendor is what Jesus never lost sight of, and *we* must not lose sight of it either. We know that the sufferings of this present time cannot compare with the glory that awaits us (Romans 8:18).

Now here's my point: all throughout Jesus' greatest trouble, the Word says He kept joy before Him. His rejoicing was not in seeing what was happening on the earth, but in keeping His focus on what was happening in heaven. "Father, I see it. I see the holy angels. I see the throne. I see the streets of gold. I see the pearly gates. Hurry up and get it over with here! I can't wait to come!" When we focus on Heaven, we also can't wait to go. When we focus on it like Jesus did, we speak about it with joy.

Look Steadfastly into Heaven

Acts chapters 6 and 7 is the story of Stephen. Stephen was a deacon in the early Church. The Bible says he was "*full of faith and power*" (6:8). Because he was so strong in the Lord, Satan hated him and persecuted him, seeking to take his life. Acts 7:54 says: "*When they heard these things* [things that Stephen said], *they were cut to the heart, and they gnashed on him with their teeth.*" They were so angry at Stephen, they gnashed their teeth. They couldn't wait to kill him. In verse 55 we read, "*But he, being full of the Holy Spirit, **looked up** steadfastly into **heaven**.*" He was not bothered by their rage. He was not bothered by their persecution. He was not bothered by their retorts—**He looked up!**

This is what Jesus told the believers to do in the last days. Look up! You see, there's no depression, no perplexity, no heart overwhelmed, no trouble or despair, when we look up—because in doing so, with the help of the Holy Spirit, we get glimpses of the glory realm. And such glimpses fill us with joy unspeakable.

I feel sorry for so many people who have all their "little eggs in the basket" of earth. We are living at the end of days. What Jesus said is true. There are going to be commotions of all kinds, but you and I are taught to look up. Glory to God!

I don't know about you, but I'm learning to look up. Oh, my future is so bright! I can see it and can't wait to possess it. Glory to God! Jesus said, "If you believe in Me, you can have My peace when others are falling apart" (John 14:27-29). Believe what? "Believe I've got a place for you." So rejoice! Look up to the realities of Heaven and be glad.

Chapter 8

Keeping Our Focus Upward

We need to keep our focus on heavenly things and not on the temporal things of this world—power, position, or possessions. We have a promise of better things in heaven, things which are lasting. What are you focusing on, the temporary or the eternal?

The Temporal Things of Earth

Hebrews 10:32 says, "*But call to remembrance the former days, in which, after ye were illuminated* [after your eyes were opened to the reality of spiritual things], *ye endured a great fight of afflictions.*" The apostle Paul was talking to people who had to go through great trouble: "*Partly, whilst ye were made a gazingstock…*" What is that? It is a public spectacle. They were ridiculed in public. What else? "*…both by reproaches* [taunted and insulted] *and afflictions* [persecution and cruel treatment]" (v. 33). These Christians went through great affliction because they were truly born again and held heaven in view.

Look at the next verse (*v.* 34): "*For ye had compassion of me in my bonds* [when Paul was imprisoned]*, and took **joyfully** the spoiling of your goods* [the taking away of their personal property]." Indeed, because you are a Christian, they will take your house, your car, etc. In fact, that's what ISIS is doing to Christians in the Middle-East. If Christians don't convert to Islam, they are charged with a tax they are unable to pay. Their homes are then taken, as is everything else they own. Paul said, "You took all that joyfully." Because these Christians knew something: "***Knowing** in yourselves that ye have **in heaven** a better and an enduring substance.*" If everything here falls apart, I can still rejoice—I know it's not over. I know the earth is not my home. I have a place in heaven with my name on it, and it has enduring substance. If you can believe this, what you deal with on earth doesn't matter that much. The Patriarchs of old, "*having seen them* [eternal realities] *afar off, and were persuaded of them, and embraced them, and confessed that they were strangers and pilgrims on the earth*" (Hebrews 11:13).

Here's the problem with the contemporary Church. Preachers have taught the Church about focusing on getting possessions here on the earth. Following that theology alone is going to fail many miserably. It's time to preach about heaven. Paul was saying: "You took the loss of everything. They made you a public spectacle of ridicule. They beat you. They took your possessions from you. And you took it all joyfully." This was also true of Jesus. They flogged Him, did terrible things to Him, and, finally, they hung Him on a cross, naked. Yet, the Bible says He set joy before Him—heaven.

In these days ahead, we have to understand what it means to **look up**, to get our focus off earth's materialism and look to the heavens, choosing to live in the heavenly realm. We need to learn to live in another world—a world where there is no stress, no trouble, and no lack. This world is called the heavenly realm. Jesus said to look up into that realm. Jesus said that when we do, we will be able to *"lift up"* our heads in the midst of despair. This heavenly realm is accessible to every believer through the Holy Spirit. (This will be discussed in greater detail in a later chapter.)

Let's look at Hebrews 11:25. This is regarding Moses: *"Choosing rather to suffer affliction with the people of God, than to enjoy the pleasures of sin for a season."* The world's pleasures will only last as long as the sun shines. The world is quickly sinking into a dark abyss. But we are going to an eternal place, where joy will never end, and there is never a dark, stormy day.

Notice in verse 26 what Moses determined: *"Esteeming the reproach* [suffering] *of Christ greater riches than the treasures in Egypt: for he had respect unto the recompense of the reward* [in heaven]." If we suffer for Him here, we get rewarded there. That's what Moses esteemed. But if you want all of your blessings here, you are going to miss heaven. And all your earthly possessions may be taken from you. How could Moses choose the reproach of Christ? *"By faith he forsook Egypt, not fearing the wrath of the king: for he **endured**"* (*v.* 27). He endured, as he had set his focus on eternal things. Moses had respect unto heaven's rewards. Moses *"endured as seeing Him who is invisible."* May we all learn to look up and see Him! Clearly, Moses had spiritual vision, not just natural vision. How is your vision?

This is how we are going to endure in this last hour. Jesus said that those who endure to the end shall be saved (Matthew 24:13). How will we endure to the end, having to go through all the trouble ahead of us? By *"seeing Him who is invisible."* We have to be able to set our focus on things above. Paul said in Colossians 3:2 that we should not set our hearts on earthly things. "*Set your affection on things above, not on things on the earth.*" We can never set our affection on the things above if we never look up. We must lift our eyes above the earth in order to see above it.

This is why we are never perplexed, even though we go through trouble. We're never bothered if we look toward eternity. I cannot speak for you, but I can speak for myself. I think of heaven every day. I think of my Father's house and can't wait to go there. I want to be like Jesus. He was so excited to go to heaven. He declared to Judas concerning his betrayal of Him: "The quicker you act the better!" (John 13:27, Rieu). I just have no desire for this earth. There's nothing here that excites me. I can't wait to go to heaven.

Obliged To Do Our Christian Duty

My life is lived with the purpose of taking as many with me to heaven as I can. We, who truly believe, do not want anyone to miss out on this glorious reality. If you were excited about Heaven you would tell others about it also. We talk about things that excite us. Jesus and the apostles were always focused heavenward, and, therefore, they always sought to lift the souls of men in the direction of their focus—heaven. We can only encourage others to see the reality of heaven when we are focused on it ourselves. I cannot get anyone to see something that I have not first seen myself. If you have tasted of the goodness of the Lord, then you will greatly desire others to taste of Him too. It is the believer's duty to tell others of the goodness of the Lord, and of the place He has prepared for those who love Him. Let us do our duty.

My family and I enjoy every temporary blessing the Father gives us (all earthly things are temporal). Nevertheless, we long for those blessings which are eternal. Believers can only long for them if they set their gaze upon them first. Paul told the Church to seek the *things* that are above, not to set their affections on the *things* on earth. If we do this, we will begin to long for the things that are above. As the apostle Paul declared (as he looked upon things eternal), he earnestly desired his "*house which is from heaven*" (2 Corinthians 5:2). He said he was willing to be absent from the physical body in order to be present with the Lord. Many Christians do not yearn for their heavenly mansion, because they never focus upon it. Their focus, and consequent desire, is only for their house on earth. This saddens the heart of the Father who has prepared a far better place for them, with Him, in heaven. Because the patriarchs of old focused on heaven, "*God is not ashamed to be called their God; for he hath prepared for them a city*" (Hebrews 11:16).

Flee False Teaching

There are preachers who are preaching, teaching, and writing that we should take advantage of every opportunity that comes our way here on earth. Whatever moment or opportunity comes our way, we should take full advantage of it. We should maximize every possible opportunity so as to have no regrets at the end of our lives here on earth. The problem with this teaching is that our lives do not end here on earth. Therefore, earth is not the end of our opportunities. If the apostles had followed this teaching they could not have forsaken everything of earth to follow Jesus.

Such preachers never tell us about heaven—it's always about here—*be something here, make your life something here and now*. This kind of teaching is going to ruin a lot of people, because they are fully expecting things that are not on the horizon for them now.

69

We have to get ready for what's coming. I say, get your life ready for heaven! *"Prepare to meet thy God"* (Amos 4:12). Noah prepared for what was coming upon earth, and, therefore, was ready. Noah was focused on eternal things and *"prepared an ark to the saving of his house"* (Hebrews 11:7). Sadly, many of us are like those in Noah's day. Jesus said in Matthew 24:37-39:

> *As the days of Noah were, so shall also the coming of the Son of man be. For as in the days that were before the flood they were eating and drinking, marrying and giving in marriage, until the day that Noah entered the ark, And knew not until the flood came, and took them all away.*

Now, what if Moses had lived for material things? He was positioned to be king of Egypt. He didn't seize that moment. He walked away from it—because he saw heaven! What if Jesus had seized His moment? Satan offered Him all the kingdoms of the earth, with all their riches. Jesus said, "Satan, get away from Me!" (Matthew 4:10). These were moments of "opportunity." Indeed, if that had been the purpose for Jesus' life, it would have been pitiful for us all! His life's purpose was that we *all* may have eternal life. Paul said, if we have hope only in this life, we, of all men, are most miserable (1 Corinthians 15:19). That's a damnable concept because it makes me live only for the here and now—let me get all I can *now*. It's a dangerous doctrine. It is a philosophical view of life that causes one to believe that *he who dies with the most "toys" wins.*

If all of life is between the day we're born and the day we die, for many that would be horrible. My hope is in this, *"that **in the ages to come** He might show the exceeding riches of His grace in His kindness toward us through Christ Jesus"* (Ephesians 2:7). This earth is one age that is winding down. We are coming to the end of this present age. But, there are many more **ages** to come, in which the Father will show off His goodness in, to, and through *us*, His beloved children. *"Unto him be glory in the church by Christ Jesus throughout all ages"* (Ephesians 3:21).

Furthermore, it has been said that God is not a just God, because there are children around the world dying of starvation and other tragedies. But I say in response to them who clearly see this life as all there is, that all these little innocent children with bloated stomachs go to Heaven at death. Jesus said of *"little children…such is the kingdom of heaven,"* and if we adults do not *"become as little children, ye shall not enter into the kingdom of heaven"* (Matthew 19:14; 18:3). My point is, God is not unjust. These children grow up in Heaven—paradise—and will be glorified with Christ throughout many other ages. The earth is not all there is. Oh, if only we could get a glimpse of eternity! We would always have a positive outlook of hope for the future.

What if John the Baptist had believed that opportunities for success are limited only to earth? We would think he was a failure, because he neither lived well nor died well (Matthew 14:1-12). He lived out in the wilderness, ate wild locust, and wore camel's hair (Matthew 3:4). He came, preached for a short time, and then was beheaded. However, he fulfilled the will of God, which was what he was created to do. The Bible says of John the Baptist that there was no man born of woman greater than he (Matthew 11:11). These people lived with eternal purposes and serve as our examples today. The contrasting teaching shows you how to live for *self* here on the earth. That's a trap…run!

There is a rich man in the Bible (Luke 12:13-21), who lived according to this materialistic philosophy. He went after the gusto.

He built bigger and bigger. He had more and more. Then God came to him and said, *"Thou fool."* God said he was living for his life here. He said, *"This night thy soul is required of thee: then whose shall those things be?"* (*v.* 20). You can't take them with you. Paul taught: *"We brought nothing into this world and it is certain we can carry nothing out. And having food and raiment let us be therewith content"* (1 Timothy 6:7-8).

Rejoice in Heaven

What I am telling you today is to help you set your gaze upon heavenly things. Live for the hope of going to heaven, and all the other aspects of your life will fall into their proper place. God will make sure you eat. Whatever His will is, He'll make sure you fulfill it. Let your hope be on getting to heaven. By the way, God favors your life with good things on your way there. Jesus said, *"Seek ye the kingdom of God; **and all these things shall be added unto you**"* (Luke 12:31). The Patriarchs of the Bible *"desire[d] a better country, that is, a heavenly; wherefore, God is not ashamed to be called their God; for he hath prepared for them a city* [in heaven]" (Hebrews 11:16). Because their *"desire"* was *only* heaven, God gave them the earth to enjoy as they waited for heaven (Romans 4:13). All of the Patriarchs were very prosperous, but their hearts' desire was only for heaven; consequently, heaven is the only thing they sought.

In Luke 10:20 Jesus said: *"Notwithstanding in this rejoice not, that the spirits are subject unto you."* In other words, don't rejoice because you can command a devil to come out in Jesus' name and he obeys; *"but rather **rejoice**, because your names are written **in heaven**."* The thing we ought to rejoice about is that we get to go to heaven! Jesus even taught that if we have enough faith to speak to a tree that it be plucked up and cast into the sea and it obeyed us, this is not a reason to rejoice. Rather, say to yourselves, *"We are unprofitable servants"* (Luke 17:10). Jesus further taught: *"Rejoice* **with me***; for I have found my sheep which was lost. I say unto you, that likewise joy shall be* **in heaven** *over one sinner that repenteth"* (Luke 15:6-7). In the mind of the Lord, the only thing that merits rejoicing is the salvation of the soul. Rejoice that the soul of man may have an eternal resting place with Him in heaven. Demonstrations of faith and power are not what we are to rejoice in. The saints in heaven rejoice over this one thing—*"Thou was slain, and hast redeemed us to God by the blood"* (Revelation 5:9).

Jesus taught us clearly what we are to rejoice about. Unfortunately, the Church today ignores this teaching. He said, **"Rejoice** *ye in that day* [of reproach]*, and leap for joy; for, behold your reward is great* **in heaven**" (Luke 6:23). The joy of Jesus was ALWAYS towards heaven and *never* connected to the earth. Even when Jesus welcomes believers into heaven, He phrases it this way, *"Enter thou into the* **joy** *of thy lord"* (Matthew 25:23). Jesus said to His disciples, *"Rejoice, because I said, I go unto the Father"* (John 14:28). Do you see? Heaven is what Jesus rejoiced about and what He taught us to rejoice in. So why does the Church today rejoice over everything else but heaven? Why do we rejoice over material things? Because this is what many in the Church today have been taught to do.

Now back to Luke 10:21: *"In that hour Jesus rejoiced in spirit."* Notice that anytime Jesus thought about heaven, He rejoiced. In verse 20 Jesus simply mentioned *"heaven"*; then in the very next verse He *"rejoiced."* (When I speak of heaven, I just want to shout, because I believe I have an eternal home there, to say the least of what awaits us there.) Why did Jesus say rejoice because your names are written in heaven? Revelation 20:15 says everyone whose name is not written in the Lamb's Book of Life is going to hell. So your name must be written in heaven in order for you to enter into heaven. Rejoice that your name is written in the book which gives you entry into that celestial bliss, called heaven.

The Lord talked about the New City of God and the new heaven—a heaven that's so splendid, so spectacular, so overwhelmingly, and tremendously beautiful that the human mind cannot conceive it. And only those whose names are in the Book can enter. If your name is *not* in the Book of Life, you can't enter heaven. Jesus said to rejoice because your names *are* written in the Book. What does that mean? You have entry into heaven! Nothing on earth is worth rejoicing over as much as this truth. Jesus didn't get excited about earthly things. He said, "If you want to rejoice, rejoice with Me because I'm going to the Father."

Look Up to Lift up

Luke 21:28, says: *"And when these things begin to come to pass, then look up, and lift up your heads."* What does that mean? When you look up to heaven, then you can walk through this life without despondency, despair, or asking "why is this all happening?" You say, "I can pick up my head, I can walk through this trouble with my shoulders squared, because I've seen heaven." Once we *look up* to see heaven, then we walk with our heads *lifted up* in confident peace. Many, in the days ahead, will be downtrodden, hopeless, in despair, disgusted, and full of fear. But you and I are going to walk with our heads held high. Despite all this trouble, you are going to keep your head up *"for your redemption draweth nigh."* As these things come to pass, they let us know that Jesus is coming. And that should get us so excited, because we love the Master and long to see Him. We adore Jesus. He's coming back for us, as He promised. When this is in your heart, with corresponding hope attached, you are not despondent.

I feel sorry for believers who never set their gaze or hope in heaven. Their whole Christian life is about living a good life *here,* with no thought of heaven. They're going to be so hurt because, according to the signs we are seeing, there is not much time of ease left. For the future will not be as good as it is now, at least not in the natural upon earth. The signs of the end Jesus spoke of are just beginning and will intensify.

In light of this, what shall we do? We don't focus on the things of this earth. We look up! Jesus is coming! We rejoice! We shout! I'm telling you what I know. In these last days, by divine grace, the true Church of Jesus is going to have peace and joy like never seen before, because the true Church of Jesus will be eagerly awaiting His return. It will have its eyes on the hope of heaven, while others have their gaze upon the woes on earth.

PART III

Eternal Hope,
the Anchor of the Soul

*Which **hope** we have as an anchor of the soul, both sure and stedfast, and which entereth into that within the veil.*

— Hebrews 6:19

Chapter 9

Faith and Hope: The Difference

Faith is not hope, and hope is not faith. They serve the believer in two completely different ways. God, in His great love and grace, has given us the vital gift of *faith* to bring us to Himself— to save us from the death we earned because of our sins (Ephesians 2:8). In these last days, *hope* is absolutely vital for the believer to make it through the turbulence on this earth, in order to land safely on the other side of the shore. The Bible says hope is the *"anchor of the soul"* (Hebrews 6:19). Anchors are needed, especially in the midst of raging seas.

A great storm is on its way, and those without hope will be driven by the waves. They will sink in a sea of despair. In light of the coming storm, if hope is not our anchor, holding us steady, we will be driven by the winds of satanic forces and sink into the sea of dreadful doubt and darkness. Remember, Jesus said, *"The sea and the waves [will be] roaring"* (Luke 21:25).

Faith vs Hope

Faith reaches up into heaven and pulls the blessings of heaven down to meet our earthly needs. Faith is, therefore, primarily for the earth. Faith is a spiritual force. It reaches up into heaven and takes hold of heavenly blessings, pulling them down to the earth. Hope, however, does just the opposite. Hope takes the soul of man from earth and lifts him up to heaven. Divine hope causes us to focus upon heaven, and consequently draws us in that direction.

Do you see the difference? **Faith**, primarily, manifests heaven's goodness upon earth. This is why we are required to live by it while we are here upon earth. It's the means by which heaven is brought to us, here on earth. **Hope**, by contrast, *lifts the soul of man up to heaven.* It is not for bringing heaven down to earth. Hope enables the soul to fix, or to anchor itself, in heaven, *"within the veil."* It provides stability, despite the earthly storms. Hope gives the soul supernatural strength in the midst of the storms.

Because earthly blessings have been preached at the expense of heaven's reality, believers have developed *faith* for earth, but not *hope* for heaven. Faith is always for "now." That is, faith is for the present time. Hope is always for the future. Hence, hope is for heaven. The apostle Peter said Jesus came that our *"faith and hope might be in God"* (1 Peter 1:21). Both are important, however, the Church has largely stressed one and completely ignored the other. Because of our great desire to be blessed *now*, we have lost sight of eternal blessings awaiting us in heaven. And as a consequence, much of the Church has lost its desire for heaven.

Hope: Our Glorious Anchor

This truth is a must for all those who desire to survive the coming storm. Here it is. Read it carefully. What I am about to share with you is a must for all who want to arrive safely over into glory. We are not going to heaven without coming through the storm. Scripture says *"we **must** through **much** tribulation enter into the kingdom of God"* (Acts 14:22).

Now let's review some of the major points we have covered before we move forward. We must understand and accept the fact there are some troublesome times ahead of us. But we who believe will get through them unscathed. Jesus promised not one hair on our heads would perish. Meaning, we will not suffer any real injury, damage, harm, or lost. (See Luke 21:18.) The worst thing we could do is to ignore the times and not be prepared. God always wants His people to know the times they are in, so that nothing catches them by surprise. For instance, there was a man named Agabus in the Bible, who *"signified by the Spirit that there should be great dearth* [or famine] *throughout all the world, which came to pass."* Agabus gave this word to the Church, so that God's people could prepare, which they did. (See Acts 11:27-30) Jesus promised that the Holy Spirit would *"show you things to come"* (John 16:13). Let it not be the case that we are not willing to see what He is seeking to show us.

Now let's review some key points from the Word of God. Jesus is speaking concerning the last days: *"But when ye shall hear of wars and commotions"* — turmoil, disorder, confusion, and terrors. When you hear of terrorists, commotions of beheadings, explosions, and shootings, when you hear of all this trouble, *"be not terrified: for these things **must** first come to pass; but the end is not by and by* [or yet]*"* (Luke 21:9).

Verses 10-11 say, *"Then said he unto them, Nation shall rise against nation, and kingdom against kingdom. And great earthquakes shall be in divers* [many different] *places, and famines, and pestilences* [diseases]*; and fearful sights.*" These are sights that will fill many with fear. We are already seeing them. There was a lone gunman who went on a shooting spree on the campus of a major university a while ago. When students were interviewed, many of them said, "I'm afraid. I fear for my life now. I was always safe in the library. Now I'm afraid to go in." It's so sad to see people driven by fear and the resulting emotional and psychological fallout from it.

It's just the beginning. It's going to get worse. But Jesus said, "Listen, there are going to be fearful sights but don't you be terrified." Look at verse 25: "*And there shall be signs in the sun, and in the moon, and in the stars; and upon the earth distress of nations* [global distress and despair], *with perplexity.*" *Perplexity* means there will be no answers, no way out, nor solutions.

These are the times we are living in now. When you are perplexed, you don't know what to do. It means that you are hopeless. You have no solutions, no answers. The Bible said this is how it was going to be. Let us not live in denial. Rather, let us embrace the hope of our glorious future.

Verse 25 continues with, "*The sea and the waves roaring.*" The storms of life are going to be overwhelming. Verse 26 says, "*Men's hearts failing **them** for fear.*" Jesus told *us* not to fear. He separates *them* (the unbelievers) from us (His children). Why will their hearts fail them? Because they will be without hope. Living without hope is a most tragic thing. When you are without hope, you'll do anything to try to find a place of security. On the other hand, when you have hope, you always feel secure. In the days ahead, we will see hopeless people rioting on the streets of America, and all around the world. Paul talked about people "*having **no hope**, and without God in the world.*" He said they would be "*alienated from the life of God.*" And therefore, "*given themselves over to work all uncleanness with* *greediness"* (Ephesians 2:12; 4:18, 19).

Continuing with verse 26, we read, *"Men's hearts failing them for fear, and for looking after* [or at] *those things which are coming on the earth."* They will see the trouble, the misery that's coming. Everybody knows there's going to be an economic collapse. Everybody knows we are headed for nuclear war. Everybody sees these things coming, but nobody can stop them. The Bible says their hearts will fear as they see the things coming—the storms, the waves, and the seas roaring. There will be no shelter, no protection from them. When you don't have hope, your heart fails, and you give up, you quit. You shoot and kill, you commit suicide, you rob and rape. "Why not, if tomorrow we die? Let's give ourselves over to all uncleanness."

Verse 28: *"And when these things begin to come to pass..."* Jesus said *when* you see these things, it's just the beginning. *"And when* [the beginnings of] *these things begin to come to pass, then look up."* That means to look up to heaven, where our hope lies. He says that *they* will be looking at all the trouble but for *us* to take our eyes off of trouble and look up to heaven. *They* look here, but *we* are to be looking *there*. When we look up to heaven, we have a hope to anchor our souls. When they are hopeless and going through troubled waters, their hearts will faint within them. They will be so confounded that they will give up on life. We have seen a great increase of homelessness in America. That's, in large part a result of men's hearts failing them. They've given up hope. But we have a hope that anchors us! The hopeless, who are able to regain their hope, will rebound. But, unfortunately, many will not bounce back. Concisely put, *"A merry heart hath a continual feast"* and *"by sorrow of heart the spirit is broken"* (Proverbs 15:15, 13). Therefore, let us not live in sorrow, but joy.

The Bible says, *"When these things begin to come to pass, then look up."* Jesus meant look up toward heaven. And what else did Jesus say? *"Lift up your heads."* What does that mean? Square your shoulders. When you focus on heaven, you can walk with your chest out. I see all the trouble, but it does not bother me, because I also see heaven in my view. I know this earth is not my home. Lift up your heads and don't be despondent like them *"for your redemption draweth nigh."* We're ready to get out of here. This is our great hope, and it is sure.

Look at Luke 21:18: *"But there shall not an* [one single] *hair of your head perish."* Jesus is giving us hope! We have to hold on to hope now more than ever. Now look at the next verse: *"In your patience* [endurance, steadfastness*] possess ye your souls."* Don't let your soul get away from you. In these dark days of trouble, in these stormy times of distress, He said to hold your soul steady, hold your soul stable. He said not one hair of your head would perish—that's our hope. That hope will keep us stable. It will be the anchor to which we hitch our soul. When the storms are raging, we are able to stand firm. This is hope.

Chapter 10

Hope of Glory

We have to get into the Word of God as we never have before. It will mean the success of our eternal future, *if* we trust it. Make no mistake, Jesus said things would be shaken. We need something to keep us secure during that shaking. That's what hope is for. Our society, at large, is drifting from its founding biblical principles. It's happening so fast that many Christians, unknowingly, are drifting with it. They are caught in the quicksand of change. Many Christians cannot discern between right and wrong anymore. Consequently, they will end up in despair, along with the rest of the world who are not anchored in hope.

Develop a Hope for Heaven

Consider Colossians 1:4-5: "*Since we heard of your faith* [the present] *in Christ Jesus, and of the love* [in the present] *which ye have to all the saints; For the* **hope** [future] *which is* **laid up for you in heaven.**" Faith is *now*, for the present time. Hope is for the future, for *there*. What keeps me stable in the midst of the coming storms is that I can see what has been laid up for me there in heaven. I lift up my gaze, and I look into heaven and it holds me sure: *"For the **hope** which is laid up for you in heaven, whereof ye heard before in the word of the truth of the gospel"* (v. 5).

New Testament ministers preached *"the truth of **the** gospel,"* which included the reality of heaven. This was in order to give the believers hope. Paul said, "You've heard us preach the reality of heaven." But today, preachers have done just the opposite. They've preached earth's realities instead. Consequently, there are very few Christians who have a hope for heaven. Earth's realities are important, but such preaching must be secondary to the preaching of eternal realities.

The Church has to develop a hope for heaven. God wants us to know it's real. It's a place of substance. It's beautiful, gorgeous, and beyond earthly description. I hardly let a day go by where I don't think about heaven, because I read books and hear speakers who speak of it. Heaven is so mind-bogglingly glorious that I can't wait to go. My hope is in heaven. Glory to God! Most of the people who have had genuine visions of heaven (or hell) are not Ivy League intellectuals. They are common people. But this is the wisdom of God. He has chosen the base things of the world to confound the wise (1 Corinthians 1:26-29). The Apostle Paul recounts such an experience. He says he was *"caught up to the third heaven...paradise."* But he says, *"whether in the body or out of the body, I cannot tell"* (2 Corinthians 12:2-4). Paul could not discern if this was an actual physical experience, or was he simply taken there in spirit, or vision. Now, whether we choose to believe Paul or not, does not matter. He said, *"God knoweth."* Whether we believe God is granting, in these last days, people to have similar experiences does not matter—heaven and hell are real! Remember, Jesus said, *"The things which are impossible with men are possible with God"* (Luke 18:27).

Notice what Paul says in Colossians 1:21-23:

> *And you, that were sometime* [past] *alienated and enemies in your mind by wicked works, yet now* [present] *hath he reconciled in the body of his flesh through death, to present you* [future] *holy and unblameable. If ye continue in the faith* [being reconciled] *grounded and settled, and be not moved away from the* **hope** *of the gospel.*

That **hope** is being presented unblameable before the Father in heaven. The Bible always says faith for now and hope for future. Hope is always spoken of in the Bible as something we are to look forward to with eager expectation and joy.

Let's look at verse 23 again: *"Continue in the faith* [that brought you to God]*, grounded and settled, and be not moved away from the* **hope** *of the gospel, which ye have heard, and which was preached to every creature."* Paul was saying that they preached the hope of the gospel, which is the hope of heaven, to everyone. They did it to give believers an anchor, to make us unmovable, to give us stability. I'm hopeful for heaven. The Bible says that all those who have this hope purify themselves (1 John 3:3). When you are hopeful for heaven, it changes everything about your life. Because I'm going to heaven, this earth means nothing. We have mostly heard earth being preached, which will produce faith for *things*. But the preaching of heaven produces eternal, spiritual, and glorious hope. It gives us an eager expectation of what is to come. And it causes us to long for it.

Examine Colossians 1:27: *"To whom God would make known what is the* **riches of the glory** *of this mystery among the Gentiles* [us]*; which is Christ in you, the* **hope** *of glory."* That's the hope of heaven. There are "*riches*" that await us. The glory of the riches is so beyond comprehension. It's time to look up. It's time to see it. The more you look up, the more you try to pierce into that realm. The broader your vision is for it, the more sight God will give you to see into it, so you can pull yourself toward it, even as Enoch did. He got so close up into the glory of God, that God pulled him, by translation, completely over into heaven itself (Genesis 5:24; Hebrews 11:5). He was living off of his hope. Hope fixes our eyes on heaven, and it fills us with a strong desire to go there.

Look at verse 28 (regarding Christ and this hope of glory) Paul mentions: "*Whom we preach,* **warning every man,** *and teaching every man in all wisdom; that we may* **present every man perfect in Christ Jesus.**" This is when we will stand before Him, and He'll say, "Come on in and enjoy all the riches of the glory of My Heavenly Kingdom." Will you be presented righteous in Christ, before the heavenly Father, on that glorious day? If this were an automatic guarantee, there would be no need to warn anyone. But, like Paul, I warn you: Do not be deceived by materialistic preaching. Prepare your soul to meet God. Again, all who have this hope in them purify themselves. Jesus gave a parable of five wise and five foolish virgins. The five foolish virgins did not prepare for His return and, thus, were not "*ready.*" They were eternally lost. (See Matthew 25:1-13.)

As never before we must possess our souls and keep them stable. We must endure. We must be able to ride out the current. Hope will do it. I believe, not one hair on our heads will perish. I believe that we are going to live forever in paradise. I believe we are going to shine brighter than the noonday sun. Let the bombs go off, let the economy fall. I see myself up in glory, shining before the Lord, forever and forever. And that thought preserves me. I am not saying abandon earth, what I am saying is don't set your heart here.

Cold Waters to a Thirsty Soul

The Bible says in Proverbs 25:25, "*As cold waters to a thirsty soul, so is **good news** from **a far country**.*" In Matthew 25:14 Jesus refers to heaven as "*a far country.*" So, the passage in Proverbs tells us that the *good news* (or the gospel) about heaven is refreshing to a weary soul. In the days ahead, we are going to need to hear the good news of heaven to refresh our souls, as some will grow weary (or thirsty) from the draining circumstances ahead. Because we are, according to the Bible, "*strangers and pilgrims*" (Hebrews 11:13; I Peter 2:11) passing through the earth, hearing good news from our motherland is refreshing to our souls. Because we are on a *journey* to this "*far country,*" we can become *thirsty* and homesick at times. But the *good news* of the glories of heaven revives us and inspires us to keep pressing on, until we make it home. The worse thing we could do is forget our homeland, abandon our pilgrimage, and get too comfortable here.

Love Heaven Not Earth

"***Beware** lest any man spoil you* [rob you of this hope] *through philosophy* [human, earthly wisdom and understanding] *and vain deceit, after the tradition of men, after the rudiments of the* [natural] *world, and not after Christ*" (Colossians 2:8). You have to be careful not to allow man to bind you to this earth. That's a deceptive philosophy. Colossians 3:1 says, "*If ye then be risen with Christ, seek those things which are above.*" Your hope in the realities of heaven will begin to move you toward it, and your heart will not remain on earth. "*Seek those things which are above.*" Jesus said, "*Seek, and ye* *shall find"* (Luke 11:9). Are you seeking heavenly realities or earthly pleasures? I pray you are like the wise virgins.

"Set your affection on things above, not on things on the earth" (Colossians 3:2). Don't let man preach to you only about the natural things of this passing world. Because whatever you acquire here may be destroyed after the storm comes through. For sure those things will lose their value. We must long for something higher— *"treasures in heaven where neither moth nor rust doth corrupt, and where thieves do not break through nor steal"*(Matthew 6:20).

"When Christ, who is our life, shall appear, then shall ye also appear with him in glory" (Colossians 3:4). That's the hope of the glory—appearing with Christ. The Bible says the moment we see Him, we are going to be changed (1 Corinthians 15:52). In glory, we are going to shine brighter than the noonday sun. We are going to rule and reign with Him over the universe, forever and forever. That's what we set our gaze upon. That's what we seek while we are still on earth. And if we live this way, no troubles of earth will ever shake us. We will be focused on *"the **hope** of glory"* and on *"appearing with Him in glory."* Jesus said, *"the righteous* [shall] *shine forth as the sun, **in** the kingdom of their Father"* (Matthew 13:43).

Chapter 11

Hope Frees From Shame

Gaze up to Heaven

Notice Romans 5, starting with verse 1: *"Therefore being justified* [past tense] *by faith, we have* [present tense] *peace with God."* Verse 2: *"By whom* [Christ] *also we have access by faith into this grace wherein we stand* [present tense], *and rejoice in **hope** of the glory of God* [future].*"* Anytime Paul spoke about the future, he changed the word from *faith* to *hope*. Hope always reaches out to what is before us. Faith pulls down from heaven, to our level, the things we desire while we're on earth. Hope lifts us up above earth. Jesus taught us to have faith in God and receive *here* the things we desire (Mark 11:22, 24). Therefore, we must have faith, but we must also have hope. We also must learn how to transcend earth.

Look again at verse 2: *"We have access by faith into this grace wherein we stand, and rejoice in **hope of the glory of God**."* The glory of God here refers to Jesus's return. This is the hope which keeps us stable. I believe in the coming glory of God. I believe Jesus Christ will come back, and He will change my vile body into a glorious one (Philippians 3:21). Christ is coming back for us *"with power and* *great glory"* (Matthew 24:30).

Romans 5:3 says: *"And not only so, but we glory* [rejoice] *in tribulations also."* When we are full of hope, when we rejoice in our future, when we rejoice in the promises of God concerning glory, we can have joy despite tribulation. When our gaze is up to heaven, what we go through on earth will not faze us. It only daunts us if we believe this is all we have (here and now). When things begin to shake, we have nothing else.

We rejoice in tribulation. Why? Look at verse 5: *"**Hope** maketh not ashamed."* We can glory in tribulation and not be ashamed. *Ashamed* means to cower in disgrace. People who have hope never cower. Jesus said that when we look up, we also lift up our heads. We see everything that's going on, but we're not shaken by it.

God is doing His best to get His people focused on heaven once again. That is why He is letting people experience it personally, because we have to see heaven now. When this predicted trouble breaks loose, many people in the Church will be no different from the unsaved. They will try to save their earthly lives. Jesus said the only way to save our lives is to lose it (Matthew 16:25; Luke 17:33). That is, to save our lives, we must surrender them completely to Christ now.

Jesus said, in that time of shaking, many will betray one another (Matthew 24:10). He said parents, brethren, even friends will betray you (Mark 13:12-13; Luke 21:16-19). It is because they will not want to identify with you. You may have some beliefs that are not "politically correct." They will turn their backs on you, because they want to be comfortable when everything is shaking. But we cannot be shaken. All that is *of this world* will be shaken. Jesus said, however, we are *"not of the world"* (John 17:14). Because of that, when it shakes, we won't shake with it.

When we have hope, we are not ashamed, we are not discouraged, and we are not disgraced, no matter the tribulation. Because hope keeps us steady. Hope keeps us settled. Hope keeps us fixed. Hope keeps us sound of mind. We *"rejoice in hope!"* But what are we hoping for? We are hoping for eternal glory, that's in our future. Faith brings things into now; hope takes us away from now and into our future. And our future looks very bright. Let us pick ourselves up and look up.

Consider Romans 8:18: *"For I reckon that the sufferings of this present time are not worthy to be compared with **the glory which shall be** [future] **revealed in us**."* This is talking about heaven. That's our hope! Verse 23: *"we ourselves groan within ourselves, **waiting for the adoption, to wit, the** [physical] **redemption of our** [earthly] **body**."* This hasn't happened yet. I'm still in my old sinful flesh. But I'm *waiting* patiently. Why? Because I have an anchor. Yes, there are sufferings in this present time, but I have a hope that keeps me waiting, it keeps me stable. I'm not trying to find support or security in the darkness. I know where my security lies, and I will wait until it comes. This Scripture says we are *waiting*—that's future. Heaven is ahead of us. Let us rejoice!

Verse 24 says, *"We are saved by **hope**."* The Bible also says we are saved by faith (Ephesians 2:8). To be saved by faith is to experience forgiveness of sins and adoption into God's family now. *Saved by hope* refers to the physical experience of being caught up into heaven and being transformed from flesh into a spiritual body. Going on with verse 24 and 25, we find we are saved with the redemption of our physical body by hope: *"But **hope** that is seen is not **hope**: for what a man seeth, why doth he yet **hope** for? But if we **hope** for that we see not, then do we with patience **wait** for it."* Hope gives our souls the ability to *wait* until our change comes, no matter the shifting of life. No matter the winds that blow, no matter the trouble, no matter the circumstances or persecution, no matter the temptations or trials, hope causes us to *wait* until He comes to *"change our vile body, that it may be fashioned like His glorious body"* (Philippians 3:21).

Seek to See

We must seek, as never before, to see into heaven's realm. That's what's going to preserve us now. The Bible says we are to seek those things up there (Colossians 3:2). Seek to see the Lord at the right hand of the Father. Seek to see the throne room and the altar that burns eternal. Seek to see the angels and the celestial beings crying, *"Holy, holy, holy, Lord God Almighty"* (Revelation 4:8). The more we seek to see, the more God will open our vision to see. The more we see, the stronger our hope becomes, because we are seeing that which cannot be seen in the natural. The Bible calls this hope. Hope sees beyond the current reality to the beauty that awaits us.

Hope is needed for heaven, in as much as faith is needed for the earth. Heaven is greater than earth. Heaven is eternal. Everything upon earth is temporal—everything—even us. This is why we must go beyond faith to hope. Look at Romans 15:4: *"...we through patience and comfort of the scriptures might have **hope**."* Scripture was written to give us hope for heaven. Consequently, it also gives us patience and comfort while we wait for heaven to manifest at Christ's second coming.

The Bible is about the eternal things of heaven. How we've made it about the earth today, I don't know. The Bible says everything written in it is to give us a strong consolation, strong encouragement to keep us hopeful. God says, "If you refuse to read the Bible, I'll let somebody come here to heaven and return to tell you everything the Bible already says about it, to try to instill hope in you." God is giving us hope for heaven. Look at verse 13: *"Now the God of* **hope** *fill you with all joy and peace in believing* [the scriptures], *that ye may abound* [overflow] *in* **hope***, through the power of the Holy Ghost.*" God wants us to overflow in the hope of heaven.

The very last book of the Bible is Revelation. It's about the end of man's experience upon this present earth. Revelation tells us about the ultimate misery upon earth and the eventual delight of heaven. God wrote the very last book of the Bible to remind us that earth is headed for hell, but we are headed for heavenly bliss. Revelation tells about the streets of gold in the New Jerusalem. It tells us about the gates of pearl and about the glory. We are so focused on how to get more earthly "things" that we don't care to read about heavenly realities. But this way of thinking is not going to be enough for what's coming.

Rejoice in Hope

Look at Romans 12:12: *"Rejoicing in* **hope***; patient in tribulation.*" If you have hope you'll never be down. That's right. When the earth is reeling, rocking, and stumbling like a drunkard, when it's about to fall apart and collapse, Jesus says to look up into heaven and lift your head (Luke 21:28). Because you have something to shout for joy about, while everybody else is crying. Your head will be up, because you have gotten glimpses of the glory awaiting you.

Jesus says look up for your redemption is near! We're about to be changed, in a moment, in the twinkling of an eye. We're about to take off mortality and put on immortality (1 Corinthians 15:51-52). We're about to take off disgrace and put on royalty. Glory! Jesus says when you *see* that, you can always rejoice. We are to rejoice in hope: "*Rejoice in **hope** of the glory of God*" (Romans 5:1).

"*Rejoicing in **hope**; patient in tribulation; continuing instant in prayer*" (Romans 12:12). The Greek word translated "patience" means endurance. If we really have hope, it will allow us to endure whatever trouble, because hope anchors our souls in the storm. If we have hope, we can last through the trouble. And when we really have hope, it's always in us to pray, because prayer strengthens our hope. Prayer gives us glimpses into heaven. And we keep looking up, we keep pressing higher, we keep looking for glory, and we keep looking for that amazing heavenly realm. Without this hope, we can only pursue that of the earth. When we have hope, we can rejoice even when we don't *feel* like it. Hope does that. Hope lifts us up above the shadows, to the dawning of a coming new age.

Chapter 12

Hope: Anchor of the Soul

Hope is precious. In the days ahead, hope will become everything. Our hope in the eternal will be what sustains us. The earth is going to be shaken and eventually dissolved. That's when we'll need something stable. That's when we'll look above earth. That's when our faith in what the Bible says will come alive. When you believe the Bible, that faith carries you over to hope. It will cause you to start looking for the future. And I see it. I see my glory. I can't wait to get there. *"Seeing that all these* [earthly] *things shall be dissolved…,* [we are] *looking for and hastening unto the coming of the day of God"* (2 Peter 3:11-12).

Hope to the End

Look at Hebrews 3:6: *"But Christ as a son over his own house; whose house are we,* **if** *we hold fast the confidence and the rejoicing of the* **hope firm unto the end.***"* That's in the future. We haven't made it to the end yet. Hope will get us through all the trouble to the end. Hope does that, not faith. So we have to always maintain our hope. If you hold fast to hope (firm), it will see you through to the end.

Look at Hebrews 6:6: "*If they* [believers] *shall fall away…*" I predict that when all this trouble breaks loose, we are going to see a lot of Christians fall away. Many in the megachurches, who are there out of convenience, are going to fall away. There will be nothing to keep them there. Paul is talking about believers: "*if they shall fall away*" because of lack of hope.

But now look at verse 11: "*And we desire that every one of you do shew the same diligence to the full assurance of **hope unto the end**.*" Hope gives us full assurance, not for now, but for over there. Hope is always future. It is full of assurance of heaven until the end. If you keep your hope firm, you will never fall away. That's why Jesus says in the end times many saints will not make it. That's why you have to possess your soul. Things are going to be tossed about. Many waves are going to be hitting, storms are going to be forming, and that's when people will begin to betray one another. The Bible has predicted all of this.

Look at verse 18: "*That by two immutable things.*" That means God spoke it. Then after He spoke it, He swore that what He spoke was real. God never has to swear about anything He says, but He swore for our benefit, to give us assurance. He says, "*That by two immutable things, in which it was impossible for God to lie, we might have a strong consolation, who have fled for refuge to lay hold upon the **hope** set **before us**.*"

We can lay hold of hope. And where is it? It is set before us — out in the future. Hope is always out before you. Faith is now; hope pulls us forward into the future. You see, based on the Word of God, we can have hope for the future. And when we have this kind of hope, we never fall away. Thank God, we have something that is able to carry us through to the end of this age.

Look For and Desire Him

Look at the next verse, verse 19: "*Which **hope** we have as an anchor of the soul.*" I will never fall away, as long as hope holds me stable. Our hope is "*both sure and steadfast* [fixed]*, and which entereth into that within the veil.*" That is, through the veil of earth and into the heavenlies, even reaching God Himself.

The veil speaks of the very throne of God. Our hope carries us to the very throne. The Bible says one day a multitude, which no man can count, will stand on the sea of glass before the throne (Revelation 7:9). Hope is what will get us there, not faith alone. Hope causes us to enter within the veil, into the very throne of God. Hope does this. When we have this kind of hope, we can stand up and shout for joy. When we have this hope, we remain fixed—it anchors us.

We are facing trouble, my beloved brethren. God wants to get us ready. It's not faith we need now, as much as we need hope. Through all the challenges of life, hope will get us "*within the veil.*" We'll get into heaven. We are saved by hope. We have to get it, even if those around us are not interested. We have to get God's Word. These things are written to give us the hope that we need. God's book is completely serious and true in its totality. It is impossible for God to lie.

Let's look at Hebrews 9:28: "*So Christ was once offered* [past tense] *to bear the sins of many.*" He died on the Cross two thousand years ago. "*And unto them that **look for him**,*" we are looking for Him in the future. That's hope. So for those who look for Him, "*shall he appear the second time.*" Hope is what will save us. Those who look into that realm (in the spirit) and fix their gaze there, no matter what, are the ones He will take back with Him. It's hope that does that. "*Them that look for him shall he appear to the second* *time"* (Hebrews 9:28).

If you are going to be content with earth's "treasures," you are going to miss out on this. If you just want earthly things, you don't desire heaven. And He isn't going to come back for those who don't desire to be where He is or want what He has prepared for them. Many have what they want—a house, a car, etc. But there is going to be a time when gas may be ten dollars a gallon (if you can even find any). Lines are going to be long. There's going to be a time when you will not be able to eat your preferred foods, because the stores are going to be empty. Delivery trucks aren't going to be able to make their runs. I could go on and on about the things that are going to be shaken. We have to get hope now, before these things happen. Otherwise, we will be terribly shaken with the others who have no hope.

First Corinthians 15:19 says: "*If in this life **only** we have **hope** in Christ, we are of all men most miserable.*" Hope is not only for "*this life.*" Paul tells how he was spat on, beaten, and imprisoned, but heaven's hope lifted him above earth's troubles. If our hope is only in this life, we will surely be miserable. However, because of heaven's hope, we can rejoice through our present difficulties. Hope gets us to see over there and embrace it in our hearts.

Now look at verses 43-44: "[The body] *is sown in dishonour; it is raised in glory* [the heavenly glory]: *it is sown in weakness; it is raised in power: It is sown a natural body; it is raised a spiritual body. There is a natural body, and there is a spiritual body.*" That's our hope—our spiritual body.

Look at verse 49: "*And as we have borne the image of the earthy, we shall* [future] *also bear the image of the heavenly.*" Paul was saying, "This is my hope. My hope isn't about earth."

He talked about hope and explained what hope is about—the other realm. He said hope is precious. He said, "*We shall all be changed, in a moment, in the twinkling of an eye*" (*v*. 51-52). Now look at verse 58, Paul said because of this hope, "*Therefore, my beloved brethren, be ye stedfast, unmoveable.*" He says because of this hope we will be anchored, steadfast. This hope makes us unmovable! It is amazing how some preachers may speak of hope, but it is never hope for the eternal realities of heaven. The focus of biblical hope is always directed towards heaven. My cry is that the Church would awaken to the truth of the gospel of Christ once again. Deception is strong in these days.

Preach and Teach Hope

Because the earthly realm has been preached instead of the heavenly, many believers have no vision nor hope for heaven. And when their world begins to shake, they are going to shake along with it. They are going to fall apart like the world does. The Church is not going to make it without hope. But when we have hope, we are steadfast. When we have hope, we have an abiding comfort and are unmovable.

Thank You, Lord, for hope. Thank You for the revelation of hope. Thank You for the understanding of hope. Thank You for the purpose of hope. Thank You for the gift of hope. Amen.

Hope must be preached now. The importance of hope needs to be explained to the Church. Look at 1 Peter 1:3-4:

Blessed be the God and Father of our Lord Jesus Christ,

*which according to his abundant mercy hath begotten us again unto a lively [living] **hope** by the resurrection of Jesus Christ from the dead. To an inheritance incorruptible, and undefiled, and that fadeth not away, **reserved in heaven for you**.*

That's our hope. It's a living, powerful, and active hope that reaches up into heaven. It doesn't pull heaven down to us. When it reaches up into heaven, it propels us up to heaven. Our true treasure is reserved in heaven, not on the earth. Faith believes for things which are upon the earth. Hope gets you the substance you have waiting for you in heaven. Do you see the difference?

Because of this reality, *"wherefore gird up the loins of your mind, be sober"* (v. 13), don't let trouble cloud your thinking. *"Be sober and **hope** to the end."* Hope takes us to the end. The Bible never associates faith to the end—it's always hope. Verse 13 continues: *"**Hope** to the end for the grace that is to be brought unto you at the revelation of Jesus Christ."* Hope is for the future, when we will meet Jesus face-to-face in the clouds of glory, at the rapture of the Church.

Paul said this is our hope. Peter said this is our hope. It makes me scratch my head and wonder, why preachers don't speak about hope, according to the Biblical understanding of it. It's because heaven is off their radar screen. And it breaks my heart. It makes me weep before God because the saints are being left without an anchor. The people of God need to hear about the eternal hope we have, which establishes our soul and preserves it unwavering. The saints, generations back, had this hope, and they were quite stable.

PART IV

Eternal Hope, A Purifying Power

*And every man that hath **this hope in him** purifieth himself, even as he is pure.*

— 1 John 3:3

Chapter 13

Hope for Perilous Times

Again, hope is absolutely vital in these last days in order for believers to survive. We know these last days are going to be difficult. The Bible says that in the last days there will be *"perilous times"* (2 Timothy 3:1). Because of this, God gives the Church the gift of hope to make it safely through. Hope is the spiritual key for these days, that the believers in Christ might make it through what's ahead and land victoriously on the other side.

Storms

We understand that hope is the *"**anchor of the soul**"* (Hebrews 6:9). Anchors are necessary in the midst of stormy seas. Without being anchored, we are tossed to and fro and, oftentimes, we land upon a jagged rock and sink because of the violent winds. A great storm is on its way, and those without hope will be driven by the waves and will sink in the sea of despair, because they will have no anchor to hold them secure. There is an old Christian song written by Ruth Caye Jones in 1944, as we were yet recovering from the Great Depression and during the height of World War II. It's entitled "In

Times Like These." It speaks of us needing an anchor during difficult times. During that time in American history, the Church sang this song to get them through:

In times like these, we need an anchor
Be very sure, be very sure
Your anchor holds and grips the Solid Rock
This Rock is Jesus, yes, He's the one

Surely, this song is prophetic for today. I encourage you to find it on the web, and let the words of this song go deep into your heart.

Remember, hope focuses on eternity if the hope is genuinely imparted to the believer from heaven above. Because hope lifts the soul to heaven, it enables the soul to fix, or anchor, itself there. It provides stability in the storm. If your heavenly Father has not imparted this gift of grace into your heart yet, begin now to sincerely ask Him for it. He will be happy to impart to you heaven's great hope. If He did it for one, He will do the same for all — He has no respect of persons. All that we have seen thus far attests to this fact.

The Word of God says the anchor of hope is *"both sure and stedfast"* (Hebrews 6:19). In the turbulent times ahead, many will wander, seeking a safe harbor. Yet, they will not be able to find it. If they don't have hope to secure them, when the storms of life hit, many people will begin to wander. They will be tossed, to and fro, by the storms and winds of life. That's an amazing reality. What will keep us stable in stormy times is hope. Hope is a gracious *gift* given by God to His children, especially for such times as these. More than ever, the body of Christ must have hope. And God is releasing hope to the Church, because He knows what we will be facing in the not to distance future.

Time of Trouble

Consider Daniel 12:1: "*And there shall be a time of trouble.*" This is prophetic for the end of days. Jesus said, at the end of time, nations will have distress like never seen before on the face of the earth (Matthew 24:6, 21). Jesus was reciting the book of Daniel. Look at Daniel again: "*And there shall be a time of trouble, such as never was since there was a nation even to that same time.*" Jesus said this as well. In these last days, there's going to be trouble. It's going to hit the earth as never seen before.

Now look at verse 4 of Daniel 12: "*Many shall run to and fro.*" When there are times of great distress and trouble, many begin to wander to and fro. Why are they running to and fro? They are seeking a place of safety for their soul. In the Middle-East, untold millions have fled their homelands, running to and fro, seeking a place to shelter them from the stormy upheaval of that region. Unfortunately, such upheavals will increase more and more. In times of trouble, people must have an anchor. The Bible says hope is the anchor for the soul in the stormy seas of life's troubles that are just ahead of us. The Bible says in these last days, troubles will cause many to begin to drift to and fro who are not anchored in the hope of the Lord's return. Thank God, because He is our hope; He is also our shelter from the storm.

Verse 4 also says, "*Seal the book, even to the time of the end.*" Daniel was giving a prophetic word for the end times. He's talking about stormy seas, prophesying about the winds and the waves blowing over humanity. These winds are beginning to toss many. You are going to see many people in the Church being tossed, trying to find a place of protection. It has begun. Many are being uprooted and tossed because they haven't been anchored in hope. And it's going to be this way from now until the end, until Christ's return.

I don't expect to be tossed to and fro. I'm not going to be running from pillar to post. My soul has been anchored. Glory hallelujah! What anchors us is not human doctrine or a Church. The Bible tells us *Jesus* is our hope (1 Timothy 1:1). Our hope is a Person (the second Person of the Trinity). Regrettably, this Person, who's the hope of the Church, is scarcely mentioned in the Church today. We've replaced Him with principles of "success" and motivational speeches. In fact, some preachers of the gospel refer to themselves as "life coaches," rather than preachers of the gospel of Christ. Jesus has been replaced in the Church for philosophies of human success. This cannot, and will not, save us when the storms break and the billows begin. As Ruth Caye-Jones' song tells us, *"we need to be sure our anchor holds firm and is gripping the solid Rock—Jesus."*

Recall that Luke 21 is our foundational text. What Daniel said is what Jesus also spoke about. He says in Luke 21:25: *"And there shall be signs in the sun, and in the moon, and in the stars; and upon the earth distress of nations, with perplexity"*—no answers, no solutions, no hope. In the last days, man will be running to and fro, because they will be perplexed. They will find no answers, no solutions— simply lost. We are entering this time. It's a very dangerous time. It's a serious time. Because desperate people do desperate things. We see this fact nightly on the evening news. But it's not a surprise because the Bible says, *"This know, also, that in the last days perilous times shall come"* (2 Timothy 3:1).

Hope of the Believer

Again, consider Luke 21:18: *"But there shall not an hair of your head perish."* The only way I can believe this is to first believe in heaven. Once I believe in heaven and am convinced I'll receive a glorified body there, I will not fear what's coming. I know that not one hair of my head shall perish. Not one part of me will be damaged. I will be changed in a moment, in the twinkling of an eye (1 Corinthians 15:52). This is the hope of the believer. So we can walk fearlessly through the trouble. As Paul put it: *"I will not fear what man shall do unto me"* (Hebrews 13:6).

Jesus gave the Church the following statement that's powerful enough to carry us through all the coming tribulation successfully: *"And when these things begin to come to pass, then look up and lift up your heads; for your redemption draweth nigh"* (Luke 21:28).

I have shared much Scripture with you where the Bible encourages us to "look up." The Bible says Jesus looked up to heaven five times (Matthew 14:19; Mark 6:41; Luke 9:16; John 11:41; 17:1). So, when He says, "Look up," we know He's talking about looking up to heaven. While the unbelievers are looking at the earth, our focus is up in glory. When we look up and see heaven, we can then, with confidence, lift up our heads. We lift up our heads in joyful confidence, while the world hangs their heads in anguish.

If you can look at a natural day and tell it's overcast or that a storm is coming, Jesus said you ought to be able also to *"discern the signs of the times"* (Matthew 16:3). Well, I look up and see there's a storm cloud gathering. But I'm not shaken, and I'm not fretful. I know the winds from this storm are not going to blow me away. I am anchored in the Lord. I'm anchored! I admonish you: Please make sure your anchor holds and grips firmly to the Solid Rock. Make sure you stay closer to Jesus more than ever before, and you will be safe. It's a guarantee. While others will be full of gloom and doom, languishing in hopelessness, and running every which way, those of us who have eternal hope, will be stable. We will keep our heads up, walking through the fire and walking through the storm. Perilous times will not move us because we believe there is an eternal place for our souls. Hallelujah!

Chapter 14

Hope and Eternal Inheritance

W e know that Jesus separates the Church from the peoples of the earth. In the midst of the trouble, those who truly put their hope in Him are going to survive and be quite well. The Holy Spirit makes the hope of our eternal inheritance real to us. Hallelujah! We're going to be all right.

Look at Ephesians 1:11: "***In whom*** [in Christ] *also we have obtained an inheritance.*" We have obtained an inheritance! *Obtained* is in the past tense. Meaning, it's already ours. It's just waiting there for our arrival. And we are on our way there to obtain it. Of course, our inheritance is in Christ. This is why we must hold Him close. Without Jesus, we can attain nothing. With Him, we have all things.

Eternal Hope

The hope that the Bible speaks of is an eternal hope. Eternal hope is established upon eternal promises. We cannot have eternal hope while we are focusing on earthly things (e.g. houses, cars, etc.). Eternal hope supersedes and transcends the earth and causes us to look up into glory. When we look up there, and we gaze upon it, it lifts our souls. We are lifted above the storms of life. Hope does that. It fixes our gaze up into the heavens. This fact cannot be overstated. Hear it until it gets into your heart. That is when it becomes real to you.

The Bible says, "**Hope** *maketh not ashamed; because the love of God is shed abroad in our hearts by the Holy Ghost*" (Romans 5:5). The Holy Spirit sheds in us an awareness of how much God loves us. This awareness deposits hope, a hope that we're going to be with Him forever. We know that He's not going to leave us behind or in the lurch. We know our future is brighter than the brightest noonday sun. This is the eternal hope that the Holy Spirit gives believers.

Ephesians 1:14, says: "[The Holy Spirit] *is the earnest* [or foretaste of the pledge of assurance] *of our inheritance*." Verse 11 says, "*We have obtained an inheritance*," but we haven't seen our inheritance yet. So, how can we be truly convinced? The Holy Spirit makes it real to us. The Holy Spirit is the transmitter of heaven's great hope. The Holy Spirit is the foretaste of the pledge of assurance "*of our inheritance* **until** *the redemption of the purchased possession, unto the praise of his glory*." It is vital that Christians today be baptized in the Holy Spirit for this reason. (This will be discussed, in depth, later in this book.)

Now what does "*purchased possession*" mean? Well, my body is not mine. It belongs to God, "*therefore glorify God in your body, and your spirit, which are God's*" (1 Corinthians 6:20). Not only was my spirit redeemed at the Cross, but also my body. However, my body has not been changed at all yet. But one day, it will be changed. Paul said all of our bodies will be changed like unto Jesus' glorious body (Philippians 3:21). When we see Him, we shall be like Him (1 John 3:2). I'm waiting for my body to be changed in the image of the glory of the Son of God. I am waiting to rule and reign with

Him forever. This is a great hope. And when we have this kind of hope, we are secure. But we can't have this hope if we never hear it being preached or proclaimed. If all you've heard preached is worldly success based upon natural principles, when the earth falls apart (and it will), your principles will be as dung. Christ outlasts earthly success and motivational concepts because He "*only hath immortality*" (1 Timothy 6:16). Look at the nations of the so-called Arab Spring. When their world fell apart, whatever success principles they may have learned became utterly useless.

Ephesians 1:14 asserts that the Holy Spirit of promise "*is the earnest of our inheritance until the redemption of the purchased possession, unto the praise of his glory.*" Look at verse 18: "*The eyes of your understanding being enlightened; that ye may know.*" God wants our eyes to be opened. He wants our understanding to be enlightened, that we may know "*the **hope** of his calling.*" God wants us to know the hope we've been called to, which is far beyond the earth. We've been called to something earth could never afford us.

When we talk about success, we say, "Look, I'm blessed and highly favored because I've got my dream car." But, believer, I tell you, every other sinner owns a car just like yours. "Well, God blessed me with a house," we say. All your neighbors on either side are without God, and they've got the same house. My point is, these things we seek to attain through faith, unbelievers attain through work. Such things, therefore, can't be that big of a deal. Before I got saved, I had a very nice car and everything else, but I didn't give God any credit for it. *I* worked for it. *I* saved my money, and *I* bought it for myself. That's what *I* did. Now, I'm looking for what only *He* can do. I'm looking for His eternal glory. Abraham "*looked for a city…, whose builder and maker is God*" (Hebrews 11:10). Of course, we ought to thank God for every earthly blessing. However, what He has reserved for us in heaven is a trillion times better. When we get glimpses of it, earthly things dim in comparison. Jesus said God *"maketh his sun to rise on the evil and on the good, and sendeth rain on the just and on the unjust,"* and that He *"is kind unto the unthankful and to the evil"* (Matthew 5:45; Luke 6:35). The point being: God is no respecter of persons. The field of life is equal to all. The person who studies more and works harder will get more.

Back to Ephesians 1, notice that Paul said in verse 18: I pray that you might be enlightened and that you might *"know what is the **hope** of his calling, and what the riches of the glory of his inheritance in the saints."* See, it belongs to the saints, but it is not of this earth. It transcends the earthly realm. It's over in the eternal realm. Nothing of earth is eternal. All of earth is temporal. Is there a place that can hold me forever? There is a home, there is a house, and Jesus called it, the Father's house. In His house there are many mansions (John 14:2). These are eternal houses! Paul said heaven is full of the riches of our inheritance. If we believed this, we would rejoice. Peter told the Church you have *"an inheritance...reserved in heaven for you... believing, ye rejoice with joy unspeakable and full of glory"* (1 Peter 1:4, 8).

In Ephesians 2:7, Paul said: *"...in the ages to come."* The word *ages* is plural. We are in the earth age right now. But this earth age is ending. We are at the end of time. This earth is going to burn and will be completely dissolved (2 Peter 3:10-13). God is going to create new heavens and a new earth (*v.* 14). Over there, there are ages. The earth has been just one age, but there are other ages to come. There are whole worlds, galaxies and universes, and things to explore, age after age. Notice it says that they are *to come.*

We are in this age now, but this age is winding down. *"That in the ages to come he might shew the exceeding riches of his grace in his kindness toward us through Christ Jesus.*" In the ages to come, God is going to show us off! I believe there are other beings out there. The universe is too vast. God is too magnificently creative. This one little place, one little speck, can't be it. But I have news for you: He's going to show us off to every other age out there. The Bible says your future is so much further than your human mind can conceive. *"Eye hath not seen, nor ear heard, neither have entered into the heart of man, the things which God hath prepared for them that love him"* (1 Corinthians 2:9). Hallelujah! These things must be preached again, because they give us heavenly hope, the hope that transcends this limited, corrupt, dying planet.

Ephesians 2:11-12, says: "*Wherefore remember, that ye being in time past Gentiles* [unsaved]...*That at that time* [when you were unsaved] *ye were **without Christ**.*" Colossians 1:27 says Christ is "*the hope of glory.*" Point being: We don't go to glory without Christ. He is the hope of our future. He is the hope of our inheritance. Those who are without Christ are without *"the **hope** of glory."*

Chapter 15

Life Without Hope

Before I was saved, I lived on the earth without hope. I did whatever the world dictated, thinking it would bring happiness. I was always disappointed. You see, I didn't have any hope, and hope is what holds us stable. I got so sick of myself that I considered suicide. I was just sick of me. I was seventeen and tired—dead tired of life. I had all the clothes I wanted, I had money, I had a car, and I had dope. When I went home alone I'd think to myself, "Is this all there is?" And then I got saved! I surrendered my life to Jesus and made Him my Lord.

Before we are born again, we are without Christ "*and strangers from **the covenants of promise, having no hope**.*" Heaven's hope is based upon Christ and the promises of eternal life in His Word. Divine hope is based upon a divine Person, Jesus Christ. The covenants of the promise for eternal life are found in His Word. If you don't focus on these two: Christ and His Word, you are without true hope. You are living like the unsaved, merely content with material things. But when you are alone, there's emptiness inside.

God wants to give hope to the Church today, so we can live

beyond this earth realm. Again in Ephesians 2:12, Paul said you *"were without Christ... and strangers from the covenants of promise* [the Word of God], *having no **hope**."* Yes, I lived without hope before Christ came into my life. And I never want to live like that again. Hopeless people drift. We are living in a generation of hopeless people. And we are going to see the most fiendish, heinous, and despicable things. When people are without hope, they have nothing to keep them steady. They actually have nothing to live for. So, their thought is, "Let's eat, drink, and be merry, for tomorrow we die." (See Isaiah 22:13; 1 Corinthians 15:32.) In other words, there are no restraints for a hopeless generation.

Now look at Ephesians 4:17: *"This I say therefore, and testify in the Lord, that ye* [believers] *henceforth walk not as other Gentiles."* We are not to walk and talk like unsaved people. We were Gentiles, but now we are born again, Spirit-filled children of the Most High. Let us not continue to live like unbelievers. Don't think you are blessed merely because you own a diamond ring. We can appreciate diamonds, but the saints will never have more diamonds than the unsaved—not in this life. Satan is the god of this world, therefore, according to Scripture, everything in this present world is tainted with corruption (Galatians 1:4; 1 John 5:19).

Look at Ephesians 4:19. This is how the unsaved who are without hope live: *"Who being past feeling have given themselves over unto lasciviousness."* In other words, they lost all sensitivity and became callous. I don't know about you, but before I was born again, I lived in the vanity of my mind (*v.* 17) and I felt myself becoming *"past feeling."* It scared me. I began to do whatever I felt, and I was becoming self-destructive. I was developing a futile way of thinking. Yet, when hope came in, it anchored me. That hope keeps me secure and settled.

Let's look at verse 17 again. It says don't walk as other Gentiles do, in the vanity and the foolishness of their mind. Look at verse 19: "*Who being past feeling have given themselves over unto lasciviousness*" (or unbridled sin). They don't feel anything, so they give themselves over to everything. Then verse 19 ends with this: "*To work all uncleanness with greediness.*" I'm showing you how those without hope live. The Bible says the Gentiles were without hope. And when one is hopeless, there's nothing to anchor the soul.

Paul was talking to those in the Church. Do you know why so many people in the Church live like the unsaved? They've got the same "can't help its." They've got the same screwy mentality: I'm not sure if homosexual marriage is good or bad; I'm not sure if abortion is good or bad, etc. They're living much like the unsaved. They are so close to the world, they are not able to discern the mind and the will of God. But hope anchors us deep in God. It secures us strongly in heaven's glory. The apostle John declared, *"Every man that hath this **hope** in him purifieth himself"* (1 John 3:3).

Paul was preaching about hope in Ephesians. He tells us that when we are without hope, we live unstably and, often, immorally. We do senseless things because there is nothing to keeps us sound. Hope is an anchor for the soul, both sure and steadfast. It holds us no matter what "winds" of culture begin to blow. You don't flow with it. You are fixed in one spot. You cannot be moved because hope has anchored you. Hope eliminates the urge to drift to the left or to the right. This is not a carnal hope for things of the earth. It's the divine hope for what we cannot see—heaven.

I have shared many verses here, and I am going to share many more that show that the New Testament preachers stressed hope. Today, preachers stress faith. Faith gets us blessings here and that's good. However, hope lifts us over there, and that's better. We need to be over there now, in heavenly places. This truth is repeated to reaffirm it. Faith is wonderful for what it does, and hope is wonderful for what it does.

1 Peter 1:3 says, *"Blessed be the God and Father of our Lord Jesus Christ, which according to his abundant mercy hath begotten us again unto a lively* [living] **hope** *by the resurrection of Jesus Christ from the dead."* Our hope is alive because Jesus lives, and we have an eternal inheritance. God has prepared *"an inheritance incorruptible, and undefiled, and that fadeth not away, **reserved in heaven for you**."* This is our hope in Christ Jesus. Jesus is our great living hope. Because He lives, we too shall live where He is. He is in heaven and so shall we be (John 14:19; 2 Timothy 2:11).

Our eternal inheritance is so glorious that all earthly treasures pale in comparison. So if the winds and storms of life begin to destroy the possessions we have here, we are not shaken. But if your entire hope is on earthly things, you don't know what eternal hope is. When, and if, your world falls apart, you will fall apart with it. Notice, please, that this living hope brings us to an inheritance that is *incorruptible* and *undefiled* and that is *eternal*. It *"fadeth not away;"* it is *reserved in heaven* for me and for you.

Peter goes on to say in verse 13, because of this wonderful hope, *"gird up the loins of your mind."* Hope keeps your mind from becoming vain like that of the Gentiles, or the unbelievers. Gentiles walked in the vanity of their minds (Ephesians 4:17) but we walk in eternal hope, and it causes us to gird up our minds. Peter tells us to *"gird up the loins of your mind, be sober, and **hope to the end**."*

In 1 Peter 2:11 it says: *"Dearly beloved, I beseech* [beg] *you as strangers and pilgrims."* What was Peter saying? Earth is not our home. Earth is not our hope. We are strangers, and therefore we're not to settle upon the earth. Peter said, "I plead with you because you are strangers and pilgrims just passing through here." Don't lose your hope of eternity, and thereby, allow your soul to begin to sway in the winds of cultural change. We see a lot of Christians living this way now, because they have no hope for heaven.

I am so thankful I got saved the old fashioned way, during the time when the old saints waited patiently to possess their souls, awaiting the glories reserved for them in heaven. They were not moved by anything. They didn't worry for anything. They were content with godliness alone. They were just waiting to see Jesus. They lived for Him, they worshipped Him, and they passionately served Him. They had ragged Bibles, which they slept on at night, with tear stains on every page. You don't see that much now. I got saved back when I could see how the old saints lived. They lived with eternal hope. The Bible teaches us to be "*content with such things as ye have*" (Hebrews 13:5), and they were. Their conversations were always about Jesus, because He was always on their minds.

Look at 1 Peter 2:11 again: "*Dearly beloved, I beseech you as strangers and pilgrims, abstain from fleshly lusts, which war against the soul.*" Always remember, heaven is your home: "*We brought nothing into this world, and it is certain we can carry nothing out. And having food and raiment let us be therewith content...Lay hold on eternal life*" (1 Timothy 6:7-8, 12). And, may I add, once you've lay hold on eternal life—DON'T LET GO! Peter said, "*Dearly beloved, I beseech you as strangers and pilgrims, abstain from fleshly lusts which war against the soul*" (1 Peter 2:11). Your flesh will fight against your soul to keep you here. It does not care about heaven because "*flesh and blood cannot inherit the kingdom of God*" (1 Corinthians 15:50). Our flesh desires earthly delights, or *fleshly lusts*, and will seek to pull us towards them. But, we must *abstain* and keep our gaze on eternal glory. We must never forget, the earth with all its glitz is passing away, and we are eternal beings pilgriming through this temporal land.

Now look at 1 Peter 3:15: *"be ready always to give an answer to every man that asketh you a reason of the **hope** that is in you."* When you have this hope *"in you,"* you are different. The world recognizes that you are not like them. They see you are not disturbed when the economy falls. They see you are not elated when some of your coworkers win the lottery. You're different. People may ask you why you are so different. That's when you can explain to them about your hope: "I'm not like you, because I've got hope. And you are the way you are because you are without it."

Now let's go to chapter 4, verse 3: *"For the time past of our life* [before we got saved] *may suffice us to have wrought* [done] *the will of the Gentiles."* Before I got saved, I did the will of the unsaved. That was *"when we walked in lasciviousness."* That is unashamed, unabridged sin; there was no category restriction—we just did it all. Notice, this is when we *"walked in lasciviousness, lusts, excess of wine, revelings, banquetings* [or carousings]*, and abominable idolatries."*

Peter mentions idolatries. A lot of people worship singers or actors, sex or drugs. That's idolatry. Before I got saved I was a pot smoker. I did things I'm so ashamed of; I lived in lasciviousness. Before you get saved, you have a carnal mind, a vain mind. There was nothing within to hold me back. Many Christians have the mind of the unsaved because they don't have hope that holds them secure and stable.

Peter continues: *"Wherein they* [the unsaved] *think it strange that ye run not with them to the same excess of riot, speaking evil of you*." The unbeliever thinks it's strange that we live purely. How can we live so purely? It's because we have an eternal hope. Our hope doesn't allow us to do mindless things anymore, because we may miss heaven if we do. We keep in check things that seek to war against our souls. And, in our patience for heaven, we possess our souls. We do this because we strongly believe in the eternal, more than the temporal. Eternal hope purifies the soul (1 John 3:3). The purifying force of eternal hope is real, and it is needed today, more than ever.

Chapter 16

Eternal Promises Made Real

Hope enables us to focus on God's *eternal* promises. In our Christian walk, we start with faith, but then we have to go beyond faith to hope. According to the Bible, hope is greater than faith. Notice what Paul says in Titus 1:1-2: *"Paul, a servant of God, and an apostle of Jesus Christ, according to the faith of God's elect, and the acknowledging of the truth which is **after godliness; in hope of eternal life.**"* When Jesus walked the earth, many people used faith to receive earthly benefits, because Jesus brought heaven down to earth. Jesus preached, *"the kingdom of heaven is at hand"* (Matthew 4:17). Meaning that heaven, through Him, had come down to meet all earthly needs. However, very few of them received the *"hope of eternal life,"* which produces *"godliness."* We are to live in *"**godliness**, looking for and hastening unto the coming day of God"* (2 Peter 3:11-12). In 1 Corinthians 13:13 it says, *"There are these three; faith, hope, and love and the greatest is love."* What is next to love? It is hope, then faith. There's love, the greatest, then the next greatest thing is hope, and then there is faith.

Earthly things are temporary. It does not matter what things you attain with your faith or how much healing you receive with your faith, you are still going to die. Over there, we will never die. Hallelujah! Here everything is temporary, there everything is eternal. Hope is what propels us over there to the eternal—"*in hope of eternal life*." Faith is wonderful for what it achieves. Faith can move mountains. However, faith does not focus the gaze upward, and neither does it "*entereth into that within the veil*" (Hebrews 6:19). We have seen that these things are the work of hope.

Titus 1:2 says: "*In hope of eternal life which God, that cannot lie, promised before the world began.*" Eternal hope is based upon eternal promises. God promised eternal life. He promised that not one hair of our heads shall perish. We will be intact forever and ever. The world doesn't have that kind of hope. Unfortunately, a large percentage of the Church doesn't either. So when this coming storm begins to blow, we are going to see Church people living like the rest of the world—scared, running, panicking, watching what's coming and unable to do a thing about it. They will be hopeless. There is only one safe place to anchor ourselves as believers, and His name is Jesus. Because of the instability in the souls of many Christians, Jesus said they would be preyed upon by false preachers offering them false hope (Matthew 24:6-8, 11). The Bible says false preachers "*have made others to hope...Because, even because they have seduced my people saying peace; and there is no peace*" (Ezekiel 13:6, 10). False preachers seduce people with false hope, saying only the things people want to hear, not what they need to hear. False preachers ignore coming troubles and cause people to place their hope here upon earth.

Eternal Promises Made Real

God-Likeness and Heaven's Hope

Titus 2:11-12 declares: *"For the grace of God that bringeth salvation hath appeared to all men, teaching us that, denying ungodliness…"* We are to deny ungodliness. It is *"the truth which is after godliness"* that brings the *"**hope** of eternal life"* (Titus 1:1-2). Godliness is attached to the hope of eternal life. Hope is the thing that purifies our souls for eternal life. Godliness is simply being like God. And God is holy, righteous, just, good, pure, and loving. Those who have heaven's hope purify themselves, even as He is pure (1 John 3:3). In other words, heaven's hope produces godliness or God-likeness.

Looking back at Titus 2:11-13, again: *"For the grace of God that bringeth salvation hath appeared to all men, teaching us that, denying ungodliness and worldly lusts, we should live soberly, righteously, and godly, in this present world; **Looking** for that blessed **hope**."* We are to walk in this present world looking *up* for that One who is to come. Most in the Church don't seem to know this. Instead, they are looking *out* into the world for the next "deal," or opportunity to network and experience monetary gains. Lord, help the Church! Certain monetary contracts could be a believer's doom if they tie them *here* and cause them to forget *there*. (Please read 1 Timothy 6:5-10). As never before, we must be looking *there*—that is, heaven.

Jesus said when all the trouble begins, *look up* because your redemption (His return) is very near (Luke 21:28). He says, "I'm not going to leave you in the lurch. I promise you, and I keep my promises." Paul said we are to be looking for the *"blessed **hope**"* and the glorious appearing of our Lord and Savior, Jesus Christ. That's what we are looking for. The marvelous hope of our eternal future is something our faith cannot make manifest in the earth. It's over there, and it's called *"the blessed **hope**."* The Patriarchs of old *"all*

127

died in faith, not having received the promises [of heaven] *but having seen them afar off"* (Hebrews 11:13). See, the promises that belong to heaven are something faith cannot produce in the earth, because purity cannot mix with impurity and remain pure. This is why those who have the hope of heaven purify themselves as they wait for their hope to manifest. For, *"There shall in no wise enter into it* [heaven] *anything that defileth"* (Revelation 21:27).

Look at Titus 3:7: *"That being justified by his grace..."* This is the kind of grace that causes us to live *righteous* and *holy* in this present world. We can't disassociate these words from *grace* and say we are going to heaven. The hope of heaven pushes us over into godly things. Take note of this: *"That being justified by his grace, we should be made heirs according to the **hope** of eternal life."* The hope of eternal life includes us being joint heirs with Christ. This means we will be ruling and reigning, not only over this galaxy but over the entire universe, throughout the ages to come. We will rule and reign with Him. When we focus and keep looking up for the manifestation of our blessed hope, things of this world (good or bad) will not move us.

Unfortunately, in many cases, we've taken the hope of heaven away from the believer. This is why so many Christians live so impurely—beginning with the pulpit, which no longer preaches heaven (or hell, for that matter). That's why there are so many drinking preachers today. It is because they have focused on materialistic things and materialism now controls them. They live for present delights. They've used their faith, but nobody has taught them how to practice their hope. Consequently, they are actually serving the god of mammon. (See Matthew 6:19, 21, 24.)

God's People Without Hope

Let's see what life is like without hope, especially when the people of God are void of eternal hope. In Jeremiah 18: 11-12, God is talking to His people: "*Speak to the men of Judah, and to the inhabitants of Jerusalem…And they said, there is **no hope**.*" When the people of God are without hope, notice what happens: "*We will every one do the imagination of his evil heart.*" When men are without hope, they live lasciviously. They do whatever evil thing their hearts crave. They are without heaven's hope and, consequently, walk aimlessly through life.

This is why we have to preach heaven again. We have to preach eternal things. We have to preach about heaven's glory. As I mentioned earlier, God is allowing many people to go to heaven and come back. God tells all of them to write what they see. They have written books, which have gained worldwide notoriety, every one of them. In this last hour, God wants to place the hope of heaven in the hearts of His people again. God has allowed a few to experience visions of heaven and to tell about it. When we read about it and envision it, it enables us to set our hope there. Jeremiah tells us when people don't have hope, they do whatever evil imagination they want, even God's own people. In other words, Christians living like non-Christians. But hope keeps us from that fate.

Now look at Jeremiah 2:25. God said, "*Withhold* [hold back] *thy foot from being unshod, and thy throat from thirst.*" God's people were running out of their shoes. They were running so hard their throats were dry! But what were they running after? They were running after the world. We see people of God like that today. They are running hard after the world. They are out of breath, trying to catch up to the world. They've worn out their shoes, trying to keep up with the fast pace of this wicked world's system. Satan drives his people. He runs them hard. Our precious Lord leads His people beside still waters, and He makes us lie down in green pastures (Psalm 23:2). *"He that believeth shall not make haste"* (Isaiah 28:16). *"They said; there is no **hope**"* (Jeremiah 2:25). When people don't have hope, they are just running, scattered, and tired. They go on to say: *"There is no **hope**: no; for I have loved strangers."* They have loved the people of the world and their ways. They love how the unsaved live. Then they say, *"And after them will I go."* When we don't have hope, we live no differently than the world. The people of God said they did not have hope, and that's why they lived like they did. They were worldly, ungodly, worn out, and tired.

Hope is what causes us to purify our souls. Hope is the thing that safeguards the soul, so that the winds of life don't blow us astray. The Bible tells us hopelessness is what causes God's people to live like the unsaved, and they live without any restraint to sin. This is what Darwinism ensures. It blocks any hope of heaven. And when you don't have any hope for heaven, you live without any restraint here on earth. This is why the ungodly have placed Darwinism in the schools. It enables them to justify the rejection of God's laws. Darwin came up with a theory of creation, and schools teach it like it is the law. They have thrown away eternal creation for a man-made theory of evolution, because Satan doesn't want people to have eternal hope. The effects of Darwin's hopelessness can be seen throughout society today.

In Darwinism, man came from slime—man is nothing. We are no more than a monkey, so why can't we do what the monkey does— monkey see, monkey do. If we're monkeys, why not do like they do? Go for earthly pleasures because tomorrow we die. I lived that way before I got saved. I went for the gusto, and it was a miserable way to live. I ran myself into the ground. I was out of breath. Following the world will wear you out. Now I thank God for hope, and I live by hope. Hope is so valuable. It's a powerful grace from God for the believer. It is a spiritual gift because it is produced by the Holy Spirit, through God's grace. It's not an earthly thing. The flesh doesn't produce thoughts of eternal glory. The purifying power of eternal hope is what keeps our thoughts on the unseen. That is, on the celestial Kingdom to come.

PART V

Impartation of Divine Hope

*Now the **God of hope** fill you with all joy and peace in believing, that ye may **abound in hope**, through the power of the Holy Ghost.*

— Romans 15:13

Chapter 17

Hope: The Father's Precious Gift

Hope is given to the Church as a gift from the Father. We have seen, through the Word of God, our wonderful heavenly Father gives a divine impartation of hope to the Church by His grace. In this chapter, I want to show you how hope is transferred from the Father, who is in heaven, to the Church, which is upon the earth. How does this impartation occur? How is this transfer possible? I now write about the impartation of divine hope.

First, let me lay down some groundwork starting with Romans 5:5, which states, "*And **hope** maketh not ashamed.*" Well, how do we have hope to begin with? It is "*because the love of God is shed abroad in our **hearts** by the Holy Ghost which is given unto us.*" This verse says we have divine hope, eternal hope, sure hope, and a real hope in our hearts, through the Holy Spirit. This hope we have from God has been "*shed abroad*" from heaven into our hearts. It is so sure that it makes us never be *ashamed*. We are never discouraged or disgraced about what we believe, in terms of eternal realities. We have a sure, constant, steadfast hope from the eternal realm.

I want you to see that we have a supernatural hope. It is not of the earth. It is given to us through the Holy Spirit. But notice, Paul says it is given by the Holy Spirit, *whom He has given to us*. If you have not received the Holy Spirit, then you cannot comprehend or enjoy the hope I am speaking of. We can **only** get into this realm of wonderful hope in God through the Holy Spirit. Therefore, in order to enjoy this gift, given by God, you need to have the Holy Spirit. Because heaven's hope is transferred from heaven to the earth through the Spirit of God.

A Taste of Heaven

Romans 8:23 states, those who are born again *"have the firstfruits of the Spirit."* The New Living Translation says it is those who *"have the Holy Spirit within us as a **foretaste of future glory**."* The firstfruits of the Holy Spirit are something that we get as an indication of what's coming in the future. It's called firstfruits because it is just a sampling of something much greater, which is ours in the future. Firstfruits give us an idea of what's ahead. The Holy Spirit gives us a taste of heaven, thus assuring us of its reality.

Paul said in Romans 8:23: *"And not only they, but ourselves also, which have* [are in possession of] *the firstfruits of the Spirit, even we ourselves groan within ourselves, **waiting** for the adoption."* What is this adoption we await? It is *"the redemption of our body."* The Bible says corruption must put on incorruption and this mortal must put on immortality (1 Corinthians 15:53-54). While we wait for this, the Holy Spirit is our down payment, or our guarantee. The Spirit of God gives us a taste of what's ahead of us, so we're assured that these eternal things are real. Hallelujah! I have no shame when I speak of them, because I am sure of this reality. The Holy Spirit is the one who gives me the firstfruits, a sampling of what's in my future. The Holy Spirit gives us all supernatural manifestations, supernatural understanding, and supernatural foretastes of what's ahead of us who believe.

We have learned that *His* hope comes through the Holy Spirit. Let's look at the next verse: "*For we are saved by* **hope**: *but* **hope** *that is seen is not* **hope**." We don't see it. We just have a down payment of it in our *hearts*. If the Holy Spirit can change my spirit, I'm well convinced that He can also change my body. I haven't seen my body change yet, but because of the Holy Spirit, I have a confident, sure hope—hope of a glorious heavenly future in a glorified eternal body. I'm walking in the firstfruits of it now. But I've something much greater in my future, something much more magnificent and more remarkable. I can hardly wait! But the Bible says we have to wait until it happens. Let's look at verse 25: "*But if we* **hope** *for that we see not, then do we with patience* **wait** *for it.*" It's the Holy Spirit who gives us the patience to wait. He makes it so real that we don't want to miss it.

Here is what we are waiting for: "*And if children, then heirs; heirs of God, and joint-heirs with Christ; if so be that we suffer with him, that we may be also glorified together*" (v. 17). Because of this great hope, I'm able to endure sufferings, in order to get to the other side. The Holy Spirit gives us such confident, unashamed hope!

Look at the next verse: "*For I reckon that the sufferings of this present time are not worthy to be compared with the glory which* **shall be** *revealed in us.*" How do we know it "*shall be*"? We have a sampling of it! We have the firstfruits of it in our hearts. I carry this reality in my heart all the time. The Holy Spirit makes these things real in the believer's spirit. Verse 16 tells us "*The Holy Spirit himself bear witness with our spirit.*" Hallelujah!

What I want you to see is that you need the Holy Spirit to have this kind of hope. Those who don't have the Holy Spirit can't have eternal hope. All of their conversation and focus is on earthly things—things they can taste, see, hear, smell, or feel in the natural. They are limited to their five senses. Much of the Church in America (at least much of it on Christian TV) preaches about earth's material things, because many in the Church don't have the Holy Spirit. Therefore, eternal things are just not that real to them. Divine hope is only imparted to us by the Holy Spirit. *"The natural man receiveth not the things of the Holy Spirit of God, for they are foolishness unto him"* (I Corinthians 2:14).

The Natural Man Receives Not

Notice that the above verse did not say the *unsaved man* but the *natural man*! One can be a Christian and yet be natural or carnal. Paul addressed this verse to Christians who were carnal. And therefore, they could not grasp spiritual realities. He told them, *"I, brethren, could not speak unto you as unto spiritual, but as unto carnal* [or natural]*...For ye are yet carnal"* (1 Corinthians 3:1, 3). Then Paul said to them, *"I speak to your shame"* (1 Corinthians 6:5). It actually shames God, *who is spirit*, for His children not to be able to perceive and relate to the realm that He dwells in. It greatly pleases God when we are able to grasp spiritual realities. One more thought to consider: Our flesh is from the dust of the earth. Therefore, it identifies with the things of the earth, and not with heaven. In the beginning, when God breathed His life into that clay form, at that point, *man became a living soul*. Therefore, man was able to relate to God perfectly. But when that relationship was severed, man's flesh dominated him with its lustful appetites for the things of the earth. In other words, man became secular or carnal. The Bible says, *"The first man* [Adam] *is* *of the earth, earthly* [or earth minded]…*such are they also that are earthly* [or of the earth]" (1 Corinthians 15:47, 48). However, when we are born again, we are born from above and can therefore perceive the things of that realm. Jesus put it this way: *"Except a man be born again, he cannot see* [or perceive] *the kingdom of God…That which is born of the flesh is flesh; and that which is born of the Spirit is spirit. Marvel not that I said unto thee, ye **must** be born again"* (John 3:3, 5-6). Now, as Christians, we can choose to be earthly minded, or we can choose to be heavenly minded; we can choose to be carnal, or we can choose to be spiritual. What are you choosing?

Romans 15:13 says, *"Now the God of **hope** fill you with all joy and peace in believing"* (that is in believing what the Holy Spirit makes real to us through the Scriptures), *"that ye may abound in **hope**, through the power of the Holy Ghost."* We can have superabundant hope through the power of the Holy Spirit. We can only walk in this superabundant hope, and we can only have the ability to believe in eternal reality, through the power of the Holy Spirit. This is why, once we are born again of the Spirit, we must be filled with the power of the Holy Spirit. (This point is discussed in depth later in the book.)

I enjoy talking about eternal, divine things because the Holy Spirit makes them so real to me. I would much rather talk about that realm than the earthly realm. It's through the power of the Holy Spirit that we are able to believe in our glorious future. And to such an extent that nothing in the natural affects our joy or our peace. Many Christians are so affected by the natural that it affects their level of joyfulness and peace. They don't have any endurance. They are living without the help of the Holy Spirit. It breaks my heart, because I know I'm talking about a large percentage of the Church in America today. We, mostly, rejoice over earth's realities, and those things can be taken from us in a proverbial heartbeat.

We know what we have in heaven. The Bible says it is reserved for us (1 Peter 1:4). It is our inheritance, it is incorruptible, and it is undefiled—meaning it's ours and nobody can touch it. Hallelujah! It takes the power of the Holy Spirit to make that real to us. The Bible says we don't see it in the natural, but we have a sure hope for it. This hope is so strong it gives us the endurance to wait until our change comes. Eternal, divine hope is imparted into the human heart by the power of the divine realm. In these last days, it is essential for the Church to be truly Spirit-filled. Again, it is an absolute *must* for the Church to be truly Spirit-filled, in order that we may truly have hope to see us through to the end. A lot of bad things are coming, but we have seen in Scripture, verse after verse, that our hope provides the stability to endure. Furthermore, we can't have this supernatural hope without divine assistance.

Last Days Outpouring

Now let's look at Acts 2:17: "*And it shall come to pass **in the last days**, saith God, I will pour out of **my Spirit** upon all flesh.*" That's the Spirit of God. That's the Spirit who made everything. That's the Spirit who hovered over the earth when it was void and without form (Genesis 1:2). "*All flesh*" is not talking about all of humanity upon earth. This is about the body of Christ, as the text will show. It's the will of God, more than ever before, that those in the body of Christ have the Holy Spirit. The outpouring of the Holy Spirit, in particular, is connected to "*the last days.*"

Acts 2:17 continues: "*I will pour out of my Spirit upon all flesh: and your sons…*" Now that's not everybody; "*your*" speaks of the people of God. The sons of the people of God and the daughters of the people of God "*shall prophesy.*" That's a sign of being Spirit-filled. "*And your young men shall see visions, and your old men shall dream dreams.*" Now why would God want us to have dreams and visions by the Holy Spirit in the last days? God wants the Church to have visions and dreams of *heaven* in the last days. He wants the Holy Spirit to give us a foretaste, a sampling of eternal realities.

In these last days, there are many people in the Church experiencing God-given visions and dreams of eternal realities. Hallelujah! It is the Holy Spirit's job to give us a foretaste, the firstfruits of what is to come. You are going to need to believe that your future is bright, because all hell is going to break loose upon earth, prior to the imminent return of Christ.

Verse 18 says, "*And on my servants and on my handmaidens* [It's for God's servants; the body of Christ] *I will pour out in those days of my Spirit; and they shall prophesy.*" Prophesying is the overflow of the Holy Spirit. They shall speak under the power of the Holy Spirit as He flows out of them. It's just the overflowing of the presence of the Holy Spirit. At the initial outpouring of the Holy Spirit in the Book of Acts, they all prophesied about "*the wonderful works of God*" (Acts 2:11).

In the last days, there will be signs in heaven above: "*The sun shall be turned into darkness, and the moon into blood, before the great and notable day of the Lord come*" (*v.* 20). So before the Lord returns for us, we can expect to go through some things. We can expect wars and tragedies of all kinds. This is why God says, "I want, in the last days, for My people to be Spirit-filled. They are going to need to have a taste of heaven as they see the hell taking place on earth." They are going to need a supernatural hope. They are going to need a divine impartation of things to come, so they can look beyond what's happening *before* them. They are going to need the gift of hope.

Chapter 18

Hope: The Master's Pattern

The Bible clearly says, in the last days, God is concerned about the body of Christ being baptized in the Holy Spirit. He's concerned about pouring the Holy Spirit into your life once you become His son or daughter. He wants us to have a supernatural hope to see us through to heaven when all the things of earth begin to shake.

It is the Father's greatest desire that the Church, His servants, be Spirit-filled, inspired, and led so that we can have dreams and visions, a taste of the world to come. This will provide what we need to endure the coming shaking of this world. We are going to see in this chapter a major reason why some don't receive the Holy Spirit; a major reason why some are not Spirit-filled—prophesying or speaking in tongues. If you are not, you are missing out on what's going to keep you stable in the coming storm.

Repentance and Baptism

Let's read about Jesus and how He received the baptism of the Holy Spirit. Jesus is our example in all things; therefore, He sets the pattern for us in every area of life. Have you ever wondered why Jesus was not Spirit-filled from birth? John the Baptist was. The Bible says Jesus' cousin, John the Baptist, was filled with the Spirit in his mother's womb (Luke 1:15). But Jesus did not receive the Holy Spirit until He was thirty. Why didn't God fill Jesus with the Holy Spirit in the womb, as He did John the Baptist? It's because Jesus Christ is our model. Through Jesus' example, we can see *how* we too can be Spirit-filled. God allowed Jesus to go through everything you and I will deal with, so we can have a pattern to follow (Hebrews 4:15; 2:11-17).

John the Baptist is the first in the New Testament to speak of being baptized in the Holy Spirit. What he revealed became a pattern to all.

Matthew chapter 3:1, says, *"In those days came John the Baptist, preaching in the wilderness of Judaea, And saying, **Repent ye**: for the kingdom of heaven is at hand."* John preached: **"Repent!"** This *means to completely turn **to** God and away **from** all sin*. I'm going to show you how you can receive the Holy Spirit. A lot of people are never baptized in the Holy Spirit, because they never turn from sin. John said, *"Repent, for the kingdom of heaven is at hand,"* meaning it is here, available, *at hand*. We know the Kingdom doesn't come through mere observation (Luke 17:20). We know John is talking about a spiritual Kingdom. He says the Kingdom is right here, but you have to repent in order to receive it. It's here now but you have to turn to God completely and turn from all your sin to experience it.

Matthew 3:3 says: *"Prepare ye the way of the Lord, make his paths straight."* The Lord doesn't make His paths straight for us. We must prepare the way for Him. This is what we have to do to receive the Holy Spirit. John says we have to repent in order to prepare the way for the Lord. We have to align our lives completely to the will of God. If we are not willing to line up our lives to His will, He will not be willing to impart His Spirit. The Holy Spirit is not for our fleshly pleasure. We have to repent from our sins and then seek to line up our lives to His will. We must have a desire to please Him, not ourselves.

In Matthew 3:11, John the Baptist said, "*I indeed **baptize** you with water unto repentance.*" What does it mean to be baptized? *Water baptism always has to do with our complete submission and surrender to the will of God and our death to self.* Baptism is symbolic of death to self, thereby, making way for a new life lived for God. When we are submerged under the water during baptism, it's symbolic of being lowered into the grave. The old self disappears. When we are brought up out of the water, it symbolically says that we have died to self, that we might live for God. Notice that John preached baptism and repentance. **Repentance**: turn to God with all your heart and away from sin. **Baptism**: surrender your life completely and submit your will to the will of God. *These two things are absolutely necessary for the Holy Spirit filling with the baptism of fire, which John spoke about.*

Let's go on with verse 11: "*I indeed baptize you with water unto repentance, **but** he* [Jesus] *that cometh **after** me...*" Jesus does not come until we do the first things. Jesus will not baptize in the Holy Spirit, until we have repented and have been baptized first. When I say *"baptized,"* I am not talking about being submerged in water, which is a symbol with no substance. Rather, I am speaking of the substance of the symbol, which is complete surrender of our wills and our lives to the Master, for His use. This is when He then empowers us with the Holy Spirit to do His will.

Father, I surrender; I commit myself. Whatever is in me that needs to go, I ask You to forgive me and take it away.

Fill me now, I pray in Jesus name. Amen.

When you do this, John said that's when He will come. *"I indeed baptize you with water unto repentance, but **He that cometh after me** is mightier than I, whose shoes I am not worthy to bear: **He shall baptize you with the Holy Spirit, and with fire.**"*

Notice that Jesus' baptism of the Holy Spirit fire does not occur until after we've done something. We have to turn from sin and completely surrender to Him. If these do not occur in the human heart, Jesus is not going to appease us. He is not going to baptize us while we yet hang on to our sin. So we see a simple formula in the Bible of how to receive the Holy Spirit. We have to repent and then be baptized; that is, die to ourselves. *As we go on, remember when we use the word "baptize" we mean dying to our selfish desires and will.*

Jesus heard John preaching this message, and Jesus Himself did not have the Holy Spirit yet. So He came to John, believing what John preached. Jesus knew, according to what John said, He had to *repent* and be *baptized*. So He came doing those things, but John said, "Wait a minute! I need You to baptize me! You are the Lamb of God! You came to take away sin!" John was right. Jesus had no sin, but He did all things as an example for us to follow. Truly, Jesus has shown us the way! Jesus said, "It is necessary for us to fulfill all righteousness." In other words, "It is absolutely necessary for Me to submit to what God's will is, even if it makes no sense to you. I want that Holy Spirit you talked about." See, we do not have to fully understand to obey, to fulfill all the requirements or all righteousness.

After John preached his sermon, *"then cometh Jesus from Galilee to Jordan unto John, to be baptized of him."* Notice, Jesus didn't receive the Holy Spirit until after He was baptized. You don't get baptized in water until you repent. Jesus came to be baptized.

Why? It's because He wanted the Holy Spirit. Look at the next two verses: *"But John forbad him, saying, I have need to be baptized of thee, and comest thou to me? And Jesus answering said unto him, Suffer* [permit] *it to be so **now**"* —not tomorrow. Jesus said, "I don't want the Holy Spirit tomorrow; let's do what we've got to do now." *"For thus it becometh us to fulfil all righteousness."* The Bible says we have to make His path straight; that means we have to be willing to line up with everything God says. Jesus said, "John, according to your own preaching I've got to line up with what's right in the sight of God. So we must follow heaven's directives because the object is to be Spirit-filled. If you say the Father told you that repentance and baptism are necessary, then I have come to do it." Jesus received the Holy Spirit by obeying what John preached, and so can we.

Let's look at verses 15 and 16: *"Jesus answering said unto him, suffer it to be so now: for thus it becometh us to fulfil all righteousness. Then he suffered him. And Jesus, when he was baptized, went up straightway out of the water: and, lo* [behold], *the heavens were opened unto him, and he saw the Spirit of God descending like a dove, and lighting upon him."* That is when Jesus Christ was Spirit-filled. But again, Jesus did not receive the Holy Spirit without following the formula that John preached, and neither do we.

You and I cannot receive the Holy Spirit except we follow the pattern of our Master. We don't receive the Holy Spirit until we fulfill all righteousness; that is, until we confess our sins, turn from them, and turn completely to God. And now that you stand before God with your sins behind you, your prayer can be, "Father, I surrender. Help me to put to death my fleshly nature." And that's when He comes, smiling and says, "I can help you with that. Here is Holy Spirit fire!" This will never change. We changed it because we made everything convenient for people. However, it is the Father's desire that we get people truly Spirit-filled in this last hour. Even if you are saved, if you are living a compromised life, you will not make it in light of what's coming upon the earth.

Let's look at Acts 2:38. Notice what Peter said: *"Then Peter said unto them, [1] Repent, and [2] be baptized."* That's the same things John the Baptist said to do in order to receive the Holy Spirit. "He'll come baptize you in the Holy Spirit if, first of all, you repent and then be baptized." Repentance, again, is to turn to God and away from sin. What is baptism? It is symbolic of your complete surrender to God. If you can do these two things with a sincere heart, it's impossible for Him not to be moved to baptize you in the Holy Spirit. *"Then Peter said unto them, repent, and be baptized every one of you in the name of Jesus Christ for the remission* [erasing] *of sins, **and ye shall...**"* This is definite; there's no doubt about it. If you follow the formula, *"ye **shall** receive the gift of the Holy Ghost."* When Jesus obeyed this, He was filled. If you obey it, you will be filled. Jesus had no sin to repent of and be baptized from. He was already completely submitted to the Father and had never sinned. But He submitted Himself to everything John preached (repent and be baptized) to be an example for us. Jesus did it for our benefit, to show us the way!

It's much easier to get children Spirit-filled, because they don't have much to give up. It's not hard for them to surrender or yield. When you are older you count the cost differently: "Am I willing to give this up or that up? Am I willing to turn from all of my sins?" There is nothing like the gift of the Holy Spirit. I am so thrilled I'm saved and Spirit-filled! The old saints used to say in every service, "I thank God I'm saved, sanctified, and fire baptized!" They were happy about it because heaven was real to them. They waited with patience to meet the Master. They were called Holy Rollers, those crazy, sanctified people, and everything else, but they didn't care.

They had a hope. They had followed the pattern of the Master. And they received the same results He did. No amount of ridicule could take it away or dampen their joy. Amen.

Chapter 19

Reverence For God

Let's read Acts 10:1: "*There was a certain man in Caesarea called Cornelius, a centurion of the band called the Italian band.*" He was a military man. Now look at verse 2. He was "*a devout man.*" This man was not saved, but he had a love for God. When you do the right things, Jesus desires to baptize you in the Spirit. It says Cornelius was "*a devout man and one that feared* [reverenced] *God with all his house, which gave much alms to the people, and prayed to God always.*" This gives us a description of who this man was. He was a devout, just, and righteous man who always prayed. He feared and reverenced God. However, he wasn't born again.

Let's read verse 30: "*Cornelius said, Four days ago I was fasting until this hour; and at the ninth hour* [3 p.m.] *I prayed in my house, and, behold, a man* [an angel] *stood before me in bright clothing.*" He had a visitation from an angel. The angel said to Cornelius in verse 32, "*Send therefore to Joppa, and call hither Simon, whose surname is Peter.*" In other words, "Go call for Peter to preach to you." Cornelius continues in verse 33: "*Immediately therefore I sent to thee* [Peter]*; and thou hast well done that thou art come.*" So now Peter is there in this man's house ready to preach. The man is not saved. Verse 34:

"*Then Peter opened his mouth, and said, of a truth I perceive that God is no respecter of persons.*" Peter said, "You are a Gentile man, and you are not even born again. Nevertheless, because you really respect God, God has a respect for you." Have you ever noticed that God can respect some lost person before He does Christians? You can be a Christian and not have respect for God as you should. Thus, God's respect for you will be limited. God respects those who respect Him. Peter said God is no respecter of persons, meaning it does not matter who you are. If you look towards God, He will look towards you. (See 1 Samuel 2:30; 2 Chronicles 15:2.)

Peter said, "*I perceive that God is no respecter of persons.*" Notice the next verse: "*But in every nation* [everywhere around the world] *he that feareth him, and worketh righteousness, is accepted with him*" (Acts 10:35). *Righteousness* is a key word. Without it, you can't receive the Holy Spirit. Jesus said we have to fulfill all righteousness. Here is a man who always prayed to God. He gave his money liberally and fasted often. He wasn't born again, nor had he ever heard the gospel. But something in him loved God. And God said, "I accept you." When my wife was a little girl, she and her family were very devout church attendees, with a sincere respect for God. But they were not yet saved. However, just like Cornelius, because of their sincerity, God respected them and sent someone to cross their path and get them saved and Spirit filled. Praise the Lord for His faithfulness!

Peter preached when he got there. He preached Jesus. Look at verse 36: "*The word which God sent unto the children of Israel, preaching peace by Jesus Christ: (he is Lord of all).*" Peter said to this man, "Jesus is Lord of all." He was preaching Jesus! Now look at verse 44: "*While Peter yet spake these words, the Holy Spirit fell on all them which heard the word.*" The Holy Spirit fell on Cornelius' entire household! Cornelius was baptized in the Holy Spirit, but he didn't get it without a willingness to die to himself and to practice righteousness. For him, being a highly respected Roman, submitting to a Jew, was complete self-abandonment. The centurion was a high-ranking, honorable Roman. Peter was an uneducated, subservient Jew. Yet Cornelius completely submitted himself humbly to Peter. Cornelius prayed, fasted, and gave away his money. He met the qualifications, which are to repent and be baptized. Meaning, he turned from his sin and surrendered his life to God as best he could. Merely sitting in church does not qualify anyone to receive the Holy Spirit. You have to be an active participator.

Let's keep reading: *"On the Gentiles also was poured out the gift of the Holy Spirit. For they heard them speak with tongues, and magnify God."* Then Peter said, *"Can any man forbid water, that these should not be baptized, which have received the Holy Ghost as well as we?"* (*vv.* 45-47). They met the formula. Peter saw these people had clearly surrendered everything. Water baptism was just a formality of what they had already done in their hearts. Peter knew they had already been "baptized"—surrendering their lives unto death—because God had already given them the Holy Spirit. Hallelujah! They wanted God! And God did not disappoint. He came just as He promised.

I'm going to show you in the Bible how no one in the New Testament Church received the Holy Spirit apart from following the formula.

In Acts 11:15-16 Peter recounts this incident with Cornelius: *"And as I began to speak, the Holy Spirit fell on them, as on us at the beginning. Then remembered I the word of the Lord, how that he said, **John** indeed baptized with water; but ye shall be baptized with the Holy Spirit."* There is a formula in the Bible that we cannot undo to get the Bible results. Now verse 17: *"Forasmuch then as God gave them the like* [same] *gift as he did unto us, who believed on the **Lord Jesus Christ; what was I, that I could withstand God?"*** Peter said, "Now listen. I couldn't stop God from baptizing them in the Holy Spirit, any more than I could stop God from baptizing you in the Holy Spirit." They met the qualification! Jesus became their *Lord.* That is, they surrendered to Jesus completely, making Him their Master. You do what John the Baptist said, and Jesus says, "I'll baptize you in the Holy Spirit." Peter said, "Evidently, they fulfilled what John said because Jesus gave them the same baptism of Holy Spirit fire that He gave us. He gave them the baptism of the Holy Spirit, and we knew it, because they spoke in tongues just like we did."

Personally, I received the same baptism that they did over two thousand years ago on the Day of Pentecost. I received the same baptism of the Holy Spirit Cornelius received. It's the same Lord who gives the same baptism in the Holy Spirit. I remember the day I got Spirit-filled. I remember the day I got drunk in the Holy Spirit and spoke in tongues. I remember, I tarried and tarried. Some people have to tarry because it takes a little while to surrender everything. Some people are so desperate that they get it—boom, boom, boom—like Cornelius did. He heard the gospel and got saved and Spirit-filled, all in the same day! It took me a few days. I had to work through the surrendering part. But the church worked with me. They kept praying over me. They kept saying, "Surrender." They kept saying, "Call on Him." And I am so thankful they didn't give up on me. But when I got to the place where I completely surrendered, that's when Jesus stepped in to give me the Holy Spirit with fire. Hallelujah!

Jesus sent Ananias to Paul to get him Spirit-filled, after Paul surrendered his life to the Lordship of Christ and fasted for three days. When Ananias got to Paul, he said, *"The Lord, even Jesus..., sent me that thou mightest receive thy sight, and be filled with the Holy Ghost"* (Acts 9:17). This being Ananias' objective, to get Paul baptized in Holy Spirit fire, he said to Paul, *"Arise and be baptized* [in water] *and wash away thy sins* [repentance]*, calling on the name of the Lord"* (Acts 22:16). Following the formula, Paul was Spirit-filled and began speaking in tongues more than anyone else (1 Corinthians 14:18).

We tell people they've received the Holy Spirit when they have not yet surrendered to God. (God forgive us.) They haven't even repented of their sins, or their vices, and we tell them: "You've got it." Well, why don't people receive Him like the Bible says? This is so important for these last days. We have to get real with God and sincerely surrender to Him. We have to truly repent of our sins. Sadly, this message is seldom preached in the church anymore.

Look at Acts 15:7. Peter is recounting what happened at Cornelius' house: *"And when there had been much disputing, Peter rose up, and said unto them, Men and brethren, ye know how that a good while ago God made choice among us, that the Gentiles by my mouth should hear the word of the gospel, and believe."* Peter was telling them he preached the message of salvation: Jesus Christ must become Lord over your life. When they received that in their hearts, God baptized them with the Holy Spirit, because they were willing to make Jesus Christ Lord over everything.

Now look at verse 8: *"And God, which knoweth the **hearts**, bare them **witness**, giving them the Holy Ghost."* God bore *witness* that they had surrendered their *hearts*. What was the witness God had given them? He gave them the Holy Spirit baptism. That's the witness of a heart being aligned with God. *"God... bare them witness, giving them the Holy Ghost."* You see, we must *"make straight in the desert a highway for our God"* (Isaiah 40:3). We make this highway for

Him to come by repenting and surrendering. I trust you have made this highway for Him in your heart, just as Cornelius and Paul did.

If you are struggling to be baptized with the Holy Spirit, it may be because your heart is not willing to align with His. Perhaps you want everything to still be according to *your* plan or on *your* schedule. Possibly you want *your* way in order to protect *your* pride or spare *your* ego. I don't know about you, but when I got Spirit-filled, I rolled, I ran, and I wept. (This in no way means this is what others have to do. But it does mean we have to be willing to completely surrender all of our self to Him—to His will and His way in our lives.) I had to surrender. Some believers can't give themselves up because they think they are too cute or too intelligent for that. Cornelius could have thought that way, but he chose to humble himself. The great Pharisee Paul humbled himself before God. Being baptized in water, by a Christian nobody (Ananias), and confessing his sins in public was something a Pharisee just did not do. This was socially scandalous for Paul. But Paul did not care. He died to his public reputation, in order to gain something so much greater. Paul said, *"the world is crucified unto me, and I unto the world"* (Galatians 6:14).

Back to verse 8, Peter said, "God knows the hearts." God bore Cornelius' household witness that their hearts lined up with His requirements, giving them the Holy Spirit *"even as he did unto us."* Your heart has to line up with God's. In verse 9, Peter went on to say that God *"put no difference between us and them, purifying their hearts by faith."* Before God gave them the Holy Spirit, He purified their hearts. How? He did it through their faith in the gospel message, faith in what Peter preached to them about Jesus. Peter preached that Jesus Christ was sent by God. He talked about Jesus being Lord over everything. (You can read that whole sermon in Acts 10:34-43.) And they believed it. When they believed it, their hearts were purified.

Then, Peter said God bore witness to their hearts that their hearts had become pure.

My heart didn't completely yield the first day I became a Christian. I had some things I really didn't want to give up. I had some relationships, which I had to make major decisions about. And perhaps you do, too. Perhaps that's why you're as dry as dry can be, relative to spiritual things. God can't send you the Holy Spirit. Jesus Christ will not baptize you in the Holy Spirit until you make every crooked place straight. It is not hard. But decisions have to be made, by you, concerning your eternal soul. I had to make some decisions. Did I want to be a dead, cool, religious Christian or one on fire for God? You must choose to be devout like Cornelius and give your all to God so you can receive the Holy Spirit. Jesus said those desiring to be one of His disciples must first *"counteth the cost."* Then He said, *"Whosoever he is of you that forsaketh not all that he hath, he cannot be my disciple"* (Luke 14:28, 33). It took me a few days to decide if I wanted to pay the price. Have you decided to pay the price? The price is really cheap in light of what He gives you in return.

Chapter 20

Believers Who Haven't Heard

In Acts 19 we read that Paul found some disciples from the city of Ephesus. Let's start at verse 2 where Paul is talking to these disciples: *"He said unto them, Have ye received the Holy Ghost since ye believed?"* These were believers. Verse 1 calls them *"disciples."* Paul wanted to know if they had the baptism of the Holy Spirit since they became believers, *"And they said unto him, we have not so much as heard whether there be any Holy Ghost."* A lot of Christians are there today. They simply have not heard of the Holy Spirit baptism.

Verse 4: *"Then said Paul, **John** verily* [truly] *baptized with the baptism of repentance."* Take special note of this: In the Bible, when it comes to receiving the Holy Spirit baptism, the apostles went back to the instructions that John the Baptist gave. All the apostles, even Jesus Himself, went back to the instructions John gave to receive the Holy Spirit baptism. You have to repent. You have to turn to God with all your heart. You have to turn from the sin in your life. And you have to be baptized—you have to surrender your will and devote your life, saying, "God, I'm ready to surrender my all to You." You have to do this to experience the true Holy Spirit baptism. *"Then said Paul, John verily baptized with the baptism of repentance, saying unto the people, that they should believe on him which should come **after** him, that is, on Christ Jesus."* John baptized unto repentance. Then he said to look unto Jesus, who will baptize you with the Holy Spirit and fire, *after* you follow my instructions from your heart.

Unfortunately, many in the Church today refuse to surrender, which is necessary in order to be baptized with the fire of the Holy Spirit. Listen to me: You have to receive the Holy Spirit; you have to become Spirit-filled because terrible things are happening in the world. And they are going to get worse. Jesus says in Luke 21 that men's hearts will fail as they see these things coming upon the earth. We must surrender our lives to the Lord as never before. Tomorrow may be too late. Get Spirit-filled today. The Father will be so pleased with you, as He was with Jesus when He became Spirit-filled. When Jesus received the Holy Spirit, the Father spoke from heaven and said, *"This is my beloved Son, in whom I am **well pleased"*** (Matthew 3:16-17).

"When they heard this, they were baptized in the name of the Lord Jesus" (Acts 19:5). Notice that Paul did not lay hands on them for them to receive the Holy Spirit until they had followed John the Baptist's formula. Now look at verse 6: *"And when Paul had laid his hands upon them, the Holy Ghost came on them; and they spake with tongues, and prophesied."* That means these believers got Spirit-filled. This was not a "repeat after me" situation. This is power from heaven. This is the very Spirit of God who made all things. When His Spirit comes upon you and fills you to overflowing, nobody has to give you any words to say. You won't have to repeat someone's words, and then they declare you to be Spirit-filled. We

must understand these things. It's vital that you get "the real deal," especially in times like these.

Paul did not manipulate them into speaking in tongues and prophesying. They did these things as a result of the power of heaven infilling them to overflowing. When He floods your life, you will react in this manner, too! How can a mere mortal receive within himself the power that made the universe and have no response? Peter, explaining this phenomenon to those who had questions, said: "[Jesus] *being by the right hand of God exalted, and having received from the Father the promise of the Holy Ghost, he hath shed* [poured] *forth this, which ye now **see and hear***" (Acts 2:33). There is a physical reaction! Others will be able to *"see and hear"* a response from you, as you are flooded with power from on high.

Now let's read Romans 6: 3: *"Know ye not, that so many of us as were baptized into Jesus Christ were baptized into his **death**?"* Baptism always represents death. Before Paul laid his hands upon the disciples to get them Spirit-filled, he baptized them in water. Why? Because it represented death to self. We don't receive the Holy Spirit when we are full of *ourselves*. We have to be willing to die to our will, our ambitions, and our way of doing things. Also, we must be willing to give up the people in our lives who are not right. That is surrender! We have to deny ourselves and line up with God. We must make His entry into our lives straight, as John the Baptist proclaimed.

Look at Romans 8:9: *"But ye are **not in** the flesh, **but in** the Spirit."* If you have the Holy Spirit, you can't also be *in the flesh.* This verse makes it very clear that we can't be both. We can't be carnal—natural in ourselves—and have the Holy Spirit, too. That's why baptism in water comes before baptism in the Holy Spirit. It symbolizes that we have surrendered ourselves. *"But ye are not in the flesh, but in the Spirit, if so be that the Spirit of God dwell in you."* We have to give up our flesh to get Him inside. You have to surrender *self* to get Him to come inside of you in all of His fullness. Water baptism symbolizes our commitment, which is awesome, relative to our walk in the Spirit. It's the symbol of us dying to ourselves—that Christ might be *Lord* over us and live freely inside of us.

Some say they have received the Holy Spirit by faith. This is true, but there is more. Actually, we receive the Holy Spirit baptism by *"the obedience of faith"* (Romans 16:26). *"Faith, if it hath not works, is dead, being alone"* (James 2:17). Now look at Romans 8:10: *"And if Christ be in you* [through the Spirit of God], *the body is dead because of sin."* We cannot have Christ, through the Holy Spirit, living within (or be Spirit-filled), if we are still living out of our sin nature and are unwilling to surrender. If Christ is in us, through the Holy Spirit, the body is dead to sin. We have to die to our flesh in order to get Him to fill us; *"but the Spirit is life* [alive in us] ***because of righteousness."*** When we decide to live righteously (that is when we decide to live right before God), that's when the Holy Spirit can start living on the inside of us, helping us fulfill that decision. The Bible will never accommodate modern-day Christianity. Modern-day Christians need to decide, "Hey, we are at the end of time. Let's line up with the Bible like the Ephesian disciples did, so we can get the results they got."

Chapter 21

Follow the Formula

Everyone, from Jesus all the way through the New Testament, followed John the Baptist's pattern or formula to get baptized with the Holy Spirit. One of the best examples is in the first two chapters of the Book of Acts. Let's start with Acts 1:4-5. This is Jesus talking:

> *And, being assembled together with them, commanded them that they should not depart from Jerusalem, but wait for the promise of the Father, which, saith he, ye have heard of me. For **John** truly baptized with water; but ye shall be baptized with the Holy Spirit not many days hence.*

We know it took them ten days. Jesus could have baptized them on the first day. He could have given them the Holy Spirit on the second day.

Let me explain something carefully. This point must be stressed: We don't get the baptism of the Holy Spirit until we have completely surrendered to Him. With some people that takes a little bit longer than others. But it is not hard to do, once you make up your mind. Once the Church told me about this gift of the Holy Spirit, whatever I had to do, I was willing to do it. If they had told me I needed to stand on my head, I would have done it. "I'm surrendered; I want it." If you want the baptism of the Holy Spirit, yet you have the attitude that you do not want to do all that, you are not going to receive Him. You have put stipulations to appease yourself. You have to *die to self* to experience the Holy Spirit baptism.

Back to Acts 1:5: "*For John truly baptized with water; but ye shall be baptized with the Holy Spirit not many days hence.*" Now look at verse 14: "*These all continued with one accord in prayer and supplication.*" Remember, the Bible says Jesus was praying when He became Holy Spirit-filled (Luke 3:21). Notice, the disciples continued to pray. They didn't mess around. The group began with five hundred (1 Corinthians 15:6). They all saw Jesus at one time. But not all followed through with Him. By the time the Holy Spirit was given, there were 120 left. Jesus had them wait ten days—ten days of "*supplication*," which is intense, earnest prayer. For some, that's a bit too much. Those who received the Holy Spirit baptism of fire "*all continued with one accord* [or one focus and desire]."

When I received the Holy Spirit baptism of fire, I had been in intense, earnest prayer. I tarried for a few days. Tarrying gives you time to get rid of *you*. Sometimes you don't completely die to *you* until the third day. Sometimes you don't give up, or surrender, what you need to until day five. God is just waiting for you. He knows it's tough for some. But if you want this, you have to do it. You have to make His path straight into your life. John said repent and be baptized (surrender), and then the Lord will come and baptize you with the Holy Spirit and with fire. Thank God, there is Holy Spirit fire for those who surrender. (Acts 2:3-4; Revelation 4:5) The New

Testament Christians were baptized with the fire of the Holy Spirit, because of their complete surrender. Jesus sent the Spirit upon them as *"cloven tongues of fire"* while they waited in earnest prayer (Acts 1:3).

Now look at Acts 2:1: *"And when the day of Pentecost was fully come, they were all with one accord in one place."* Hallelujah! Verse 4: *"And they were all filled with the Holy Ghost, and began to speak with other tongues."* I want you to notice that Jesus gave them John's formula to follow. In every case in the New Testament when it talks about being Spirit-filled, it always goes back to what John said. This is the pattern that Jesus fulfilled, and He is our example. When we follow this pattern, we *shall* be Spirit-filled. There's no doubt about it!

Let's look at verse 13: *"Others mocking…"* When the disciples were Spirit-filled, people started poking fun at them. They insulted them by calling them names and saying they were drunk, stupid, and acting like fools. Some mocked them and said, *"These men are full of new wine."* Peter says, *"For these are not drunken, as ye suppose, seeing it is but the third hour of the day* [9 a.m.]" (*v.* 15).

Here's what I want you to see: In order for these believers to become Spirit-filled, they were willing to become a public spectacle. Some Christians will never get truly Spirit-filled because they are not willing to be laughed at. Their self-image, their sense of personal dignity, and their stubborn pride will always cause them to back away from the greater things of God. I'm telling you the truth, and we must not change the truth. We need to teach our children that they need to surrender. Just because you mumble some words doesn't mean you are Spirit baptized. This is a thing from heaven I'm talking about. It's truly a supernatural experience. Concerning those in the upper-room, the Bible says their experience was *"from heaven."*

In these last days, the heavenly Father desires to pour out His Spirit upon all in the Church. If you are a part of the Church and have not been baptized with the Holy Spirit, as we have seen in Scripture, you can be. All you need is an open and surrendered heart. Ask the Father for this heavenly experience. He will give it to you. All who ask receive: *"Your heavenly Father* [will] *give the Holy Spirit to them that ask Him"* (Luke 11:13). It is interesting to note that before Jesus encouraged us to ask for the Holy Spirit, He first said to ask, *"Forgive us our sins"* (v. 4). He also said to ask, *"Thy kingdom come, Thy will be done"* (v. 2), meaning yield to the Father's will. Again we see the Holy Spirit is given after sin is dealt with and surrender is made.

Acts 5:31 says, *"Him hath God exalted with his right hand to be a Prince and a Saviour, for to give **repentance** to Israel, and forgiveness of sins."* You don't get the Holy Spirit until you repent and turn from sin. Now verse 32: *"And we are his witnesses of these things; and so is also the Holy Ghost, **whom God hath given to them that obey him**."* We say receive the Holy Spirit by faith. The Word says we receive the Holy Spirit by obeying Him. Both are right and necessary. Peter said Jesus gives the Holy Spirit to all those who obey Him. The first thing we must obey is the command to repent. The second thing is baptism (or surrender). The Bible talks about the *"obedience of faith"* (Romans 16:26), and there is no *true* faith apart from obedience (James 2:17, 20-23, 26).

Look at Mark 16:16. Jesus says: *"He that **believeth** and is **baptized** shall be saved."* Peter said Jesus came *"to give **repentance**."* In order to receive the Holy Spirit baptism, you have to obey both— repentance and baptism, meaning die to *you* and completely surrender to *Him*. Notice the last phrase of verse 17, Jesus said: *"They shall speak with new tongues."* That's the Holy Spirit baptism. Jesus says you don't get the Holy Spirit baptism unless you are baptized in water (or completely surrender first). That's not just being wet. That means we have to surrender our lives. I have to die to *me*. Peter says if we obey what He says, we will receive the Holy Spirit baptism.

There are many people in church who don't have the Holy Spirit, because they've never lined up with God's Word. They've tried to get the Holy Spirit without lining up first. If we do what the Bible says, *boom*! He'll come and baptize us. The Church needs to know these things, especially, in light of the times we are living in. Many have been taught that as a Christian, they automatically have the Holy Spirit baptism. However, we see Scripture teaches differently from that. (Being born again of the Spirit, yes. Being baptized in the fire of the Spirit, no. The latter is a separate experience of grace.)

Acts 8:13 says: *"Then Simon himself **believed** also: and when he was **baptized**, he continued with Philip."* This is a disciple called Simon who believed and was baptized. The point here is that you also have to *repent*. Many people get baptized in water without repenting, which means their baptism was one of a dry sinner who came up out of the water a wet sinner. Nothing has really changed in their heart. Simon was baptized in water. Now look at verses 15 through 17:

> *Who, when they* [Peter and John] *were come down, prayed for them [the new believers], that they might receive the Holy Ghost: (For as yet he was fallen upon none of them: only they were baptized in the name of the Lord Jesus.) Then laid they their hands on them, and they received the Holy Ghost.*

Now verse 18: *"And when Simon saw that through laying on of the apostles' hands the Holy Ghost was given, he offered them money."*

Notice that Simon was the only one among the new believers who didn't receive the Holy Spirit. So he figured he could buy the Spirit of God with money. Why wasn't he filled with the Holy Spirit like the rest of them? It's because he didn't meet the qualifications. Look at verse 21. Peter says to Simon, *"Thou hast neither part nor lot in this matter: for **thy heart is not right** in the sight of God."* Remember, God bears witness with a person's heart when He imparts the Holy Spirit. Just because Simon was baptized in water doesn't mean he had *repented* of his sins. His heart wasn't right, and he didn't receive the Holy Spirit when the rest of them did. We have to get our hearts right. We must truly repent of ours sins, sincerely from our hearts.

Now look at verse 22 and notice what Peter said to Simon: *"Repent."* What did he do in verse 13? He was *baptized.* But you have to do something else first—*repent.* This pattern is throughout all the Scripture concerning the Holy Spirit infilling. We have to do both: turn from our sins to God and then surrender ourselves completely. Peter said, *"**Repent** therefore of this thy wickedness"* (*v.* 22). Peter tells Simon, "You don't have any part in this Holy Spirit baptism because your heart isn't right." Peter knew if God baptized everybody in the Holy Spirit but Simon, there was something not right in him. Peter knew this because the formula, or the pattern for receiving the Holy Spirit baptism, works.

Let's read one more passage of Scripture. Jude is a book about the end-times, warning the Church of ungodly men in the midst. Jude 1:12 says *"clouds they are without water."* That means they don't have the Holy Spirit. In verse 18, Jude reminds the believers that the apostles had warned them about mockers *"who should walk after their own ungodly lusts."* These are people in the Church, walking after their own lusts. They want to be in Church and say they are saved, but they remain in their sin. Now look at verse 19: *"These be they who separate themselves, sensual* [carnal, fleshly], ***having not the Spirit*****.**" See, again, until we give up the flesh, we can't receive the Holy Spirit baptism.

These are the last days. The Bible says many are not going to have the Holy Spirit. This is the greatest gift God wants the church to have in these last days. Make the decision to follow the truth and make the way straight for God. If you follow the formula—repent and be baptized—you will receive the Holy Spirit with all the benefits and privileges, especially *the impartation of divine hope.*

Victorious Living

So, how will we experience *victorious living* in these troublesome times, and the even more perilous times to come? We must have divine hope. Jesus is our hope of glory. He is our soon coming King!

Remember, we don't get hope by looking around at what is happening on the earth. We get hope by *looking up* to the wonderful things that await us in heaven. We get hope by keeping our focus in the heavens and thinking on the amazing things God has in store for us there. These things are eternal promises given to us by a God, who can be trusted to keep His Word. He does not lie or change His mind. They are certain. They *will* come to pass. We will live with Him forever in paradise. He promised!

Let us meditate on these things and hide them in our hearts. Purpose to think on heavenly things. Focus on God and His promises. They will bring forth hope in your heart and mind, causing God's peace to surround you. You will not be troubled any longer by the things on the earth. You know they are temporary. You are fixed on what is eternal. No matter what happens, you will remain steadfast and sure, because you have decided to surrender completely to God. You are filled with God's presence and joy.

Beyond believing in faith for the present, let us rest in hope for the future. Faith brought us to God and His salvation, through Jesus Christ, by His love and grace. Hope is what anchors us until the end. Hope stabilizes us so we can walk with sure footing on the straight and narrow path He has set before us, which leads us into His loving, everlasting Kingdom.

Divine hope—heaven's hope—is imparted to us by the Holy Spirit. We need to have the Holy Spirit within us to embrace and enjoy this amazing hope. This is why the Father and the Son are eager to baptize us in the fire of the Holy Spirit, especially now. We achieve this as we follow the pattern Jesus followed to be baptized in the Holy Spirit. Let us repent of our sins, die to ourselves, and ask Jesus to baptize us afresh in His Holy Spirit. Father, we now embrace the Holy Spirit and all He has to offer us. We ask in faith to be Spirit-filled. Amen.

My desire for the Church is that it experiences this hope—that it might see it, embrace it, live in the light of it, nurture it, and teach it to others, so that we can all thrive and live joyously as *"that day"* draws near. My desire is that we live victoriously through divine hope, looking up and lifting our heads until the Lord comes.

Thank You for Your Holy Spirit, Father, which You give to us in love, through Your Son, Jesus Christ. Thank You for the hope, which Your Holy Spirit brings that anchors us. Thank You for the comfort, joy, and peace we have as we keep our eyes on You and the hope of a home forever with You. We give You all the praise, the honor, and the glory. In Jesus' name, Amen.

Appendix

Finally: A Thought About America

Is There Hope for her?

I do not believe God is going to abandon the great nation of America. This land and its people were dedicated to God by the founding fathers. According to Scripture, God does many things for the sake of the founding fathers of a land. For instance: *"As touching the election* [God's chosen people], *they are beloved* [or especially loved] **for the father's sake"**…*"We declare unto you glad tidings how the promise which was made **unto the fathers**, God hath fulfilled the same unto their children"* (Romans 11:28, Acts 13:32-33).

In 1607 the original settlers of the new land we now call America, knelt down in the sand by a wooden Cross they had erected and dedicated this land to God. This what they prayed:

We do hereby dedicate this, land and ourselves, to reach the people within these shores with the gospel of Jesus Christ, and to raise up godly generations after us, and with these generations take the Kingdom of God to all the earth.

This is one example of many, which shows the heart of the founding fathers of this great nation.

The apostle Paul declared he was *"persuaded that he [God] is able to keep* [guard and protect] *that which I have committed unto him"* (2 Timothy 1:12). Because Paul had *"committed"* his life to God, he also declared, *"The Lord shall deliver me from every evil work, and **will preserve** me"* (2 Timothy 4:18). Because America, from its inception, had been committed to God, I am persuaded that He is able to keep her. Therefore, we can declare like Paul: *"The Lord shall deliver and preserve this great land that is His."*

However, because of God's care for America and its people, He will *discipline* and *correct* us. Both are very necessary today to save us from ourselves. As a people, we must commit to Him again.

The Bible says of all people upon earth, *"Destruction and misery are in their ways: And the way of peace they have not known"* (Romans 3:16-17). Therefore, if God chose to leave us to ourselves, we could not survive as a great nation. All people left to themselves are self-destructive. We are making ourselves miserable in America, and we will, ultimately, destroy ourselves as a people if God does not intervene. There are people who *"professing **themselves** to be wise,* [but] *they become fools...Wherefore, God also gave them up to uncleanness"* (Romans 1:22, 24).

The worst thing that can happen to any people is to be given up by God to run after their own *uncleanness*. Man tends only to self-imposed misery because *"There is none that seeketh after God"* (Romans 3:11). We must understand that all goodness in the earth comes from God. Jesus said, *"There is none good but one, that is, God"* (Mark 10:18). America can only be good again as she seeks the face of God once again.

I am assured of God's love for America. And in His loving care, He is allowing affliction to come upon this land. Because when His people are afflicted with great troubles and trials, they seek Him. And *only* in seeking Him, can we be restored back to His goodness as a nation. Affliction restores us to goodness. Affliction humbles us. It brings us back into God's favor. God *"giveth grace to the humble"* (James 4:6). God lifts up the humble and sets them on high. But He brings down the proud.

For instance, the early 1920s in America was called The Roaring Twenties. It was a time of great economic prosperity with the stock market at an all-time high. It was a time of care-free living, with all the vices that accompany such. Notwithstanding, The Roaring Twenties ended with The Great Depression of 1929. Prominent men in three piece suits stood in long soup lines just to eat. What a crash! However, this great crash led to a spiritual revival and an awakening to morality and modesty in American once again.

"Ephraim [God's people] *is oppressed and broken"* (Hosea 5:11). God says, *"In their affliction they will seek me early* [or earnestly]" (*v.* 15). Then, as God's people began to seek the face of God once again because of their affliction, they declared of God: *"He shall come unto us as the rain, as the latter and former rain unto the earth"* (Hosea 6:3). This speaks of the return of God's goodness to His people once again.

The latter and former rain speaks of His abundant favor and increase of blessings throughout the land. The blessings only returned when God's people earnestly sought Him because of their affliction. I am convinced that this is how it shall be with us. After 9/11, for a brief time, Americans darkened the doors of churches, humbly seeking the face of God. Greater afflictions are coming that we might pray more earnestly to God for His mercy and forgiveness.

Because of God's loving care for America, night *must* come before the dawning of a new day over this great land. Thus, we understand why David could say, *"It is good for me that I have been afflicted"* (Psalm 119:71). And Job could say, *"The Lord gave, and the Lord hath taken away; blessed be the name of the Lord"* (Job 1:21). There can be great blessings hidden in affliction and when things of this earth are taken away.

Without debate, God has greatly prospered America, this great Christian land. (The Western world has prospered because of its great religious heritage.) We have received many material blessings. Notwithstanding, we must be mindful of the fact that God's chosen people, the nation of Israel, whom He greatly loves, was ALWAYS prosperous before the judgment of God came upon them. In fact, Israel's prosperity was always a part of why God would, ultimately, *discipline* and seek to *correct* them.

In Israel's abundance, they became prideful and conceited (as America has now become), assuming their own *wisdom* and *might* were the reasons for their blessings. Therefore, God would diminish their blessings, through different afflictions, to humble them, seeking to bring them back to Himself. This process of godly correction has already begun with us.

As with ancient Israel, so with modern America, the **only hope** of restoration to greatness is in our returning to the God of our fathers. Oh God, please turn us again to You! As the Word of the Lord declares: *"Turn us back to you, O Lord, and we will be restored"* (Lamentations 5:21, NKJV).

AMERICA WILL RETURN TO GOD! A spiritual awakening is coming to America—by the grace of her loving God. However, let me be swift to reiterate, this awakening will not come without pain. Our heavenly Father declares:

Whom the Lord loveth he chasteneth....Now no chastening for the present seemeth to be joyous, but grievous: nevertheless afterward it yieldeth the peaceable fruit of righteousness. (Hebrews 12:6, 11)

GOD BLESS AMERICA!

The Lord told Israel in Deuteronomy chapter 11 that *He* would give them "*a land that floweth with milk and honey*" (*v.* 9). Then He told them, "*Take heed to yourselves, that your heart be not deceived*" (*v.* 16), in pridefully thinking, you have blessed yourselves through your own wisdom and might. God told them, if they did take the credit for *His* goodness to them, "*then the LORD's wrath be kindled against you*" (*v.* 17). God warned Israel that if they were not careful, they could go from His blessings to His discipline.

Often, in Scripture, prosperity is what triggers judgment. In that, prosperity can cause a great people to become arrogantly conceited, as was the case with Rome, Babylon, Egypt, etc. In each case, their pride became their ruin. America is now headed in this same direction.

Behold, this was the iniquity of thy sister, Sodom: pride [and] fullness of bread...And they were haughty... therefore I took them away as I saw good. (Ezekiel 16:49-50)

In the above passage, and others, God warned *His* people about the dangers of prosperity, before *He* ever prospered them. We preachers today, all too often, have failed to warn God's people about the potential downside in the blessing of abundance. The Lord warned Israel again and again:

> *When thy herds and thy flocks multiply, and thy silver and thy gold is multiplied, and all that thou hast is multiplied;* **Then** *thine heart be lifted up and thou forget the LORD thy God….And thou say in thine heart, My power and the might of mine hand hath gotten me this wealth. But thou shall remember the LORD thy God: for it is he that giveth thee power to get wealth.* (Deuteronomy 8:13-14, 17-18)

Our loving, heavenly Father never hesitated to warn His people of this potential danger. (Please read 1 Timothy 6:8-10.)

New Testament ministers admonished:

> *As for the rich in this world,* **charge** *them not to be proud and arrogant and contemptuous of others, nor to set their* **hopes** *on uncertain riches, but on God: Who richly and ceaselessly provides us with everything for [our] enjoyment.* (1 Timothy 6:17, AMP)

This verse clearly does not condemn wealth. We are to enjoy all the riches of God's generosity towards us. He gives earthly blessings for our natural benefit and pleasure. However, this Scripture does *warn* us about the dangers wealth can cause. Wealth can create pride in the unguarded human spirit. Then, *"God resisteth the proud…Ye rich men, weep and howl for your miseries that shall come upon you"* (James 4:6; 5:1).

Mary, the Mother of Jesus, declared: *"The rich he hath sent empty away"* (Luke 1:53). First, why are the rich empty? Because wealth and the things of wealth cannot fill the void in one's heart. Second, why does God send the wealthy away empty? Because the rich have a tendency to put their trust in *the things they possess,* and, therefore, do not hunger for *the things of God.* But Mary declared of herself: *"He hath filled the **hungry** with good things."* Jesus spoke of *"the deceitfulness of riches"* (Mark 4:19). I believe the prosperity of America has deceived her, and it has caused her to lose her hunger for the true and living God.

Jesus further warned, *"Take heed, and **beware** of covetousness: for a man's life consisteth not in the abundance of the things which he possesseth"* (Luke 12:15). We have all seen wealthy celebrities whose lives are so empty. Fullness of life only comes through a right relationship with God and a proper focus on the eternal. Jesus, knowing the power wealth can have on people, said it would be difficult for a rich man to get into the Kingdom of heaven (Matthew 19:23).

Hunger is a sign of good health, both naturally and spiritually. The rich tend not to be hungry for the things of God because of their overabundance of material things, which meet all their earthly needs. Therefore, they also have a tendency to be spiritually unhealthy. Point being: if we are not CAREFUL, our "toys" can distract us from God, without us even realizing it. The more we have, the more potential for distraction there is. Therefore, the more we attain in this life, the more determined we should be to seek God's face. Jesus said, *"Blessed be ye poor: for yours is the kingdom of God. Blessed are ye that hunger now: for ye shall be filled"* (Luke 6:20-21). *"Blessed are the poor in spirit; for theirs is the kingdom of heaven"* (Matthew 5:3). Paul said,

> *[The] desolate has fixed her **hope** on God and perseveres in supplications and prayers night and day, whereas she who lives in pleasure and self-gratification [giving herself up to luxury and self-indulgence] is dead even while she [still] lives.* (1 Timothy 5:5-6, AMP)

Wealth is not evil in and of itself. However, if we are not *careful,* wealth can rob us of our hunger for God, thereby, rendering us empty inside.

Again, I emphasize, God is not against wealth by any means— heaven is the epitome of abundance. That withstanding, the Bible tells us of the heart of man upon earth: *"The heart is deceitful above all things, and desperately wicked"* (Jeremiah 17:9). Because of this fact, God is against what wealth can do to the heart of man upon earth. This is why God instructs us: *"Keep thy heart with all diligence"* (Proverbs 4:23).

Oh! If only more of the preachers would have warned America! We could have avoided so much of what is coming to humble us! Preaching prosperity is desirable and good. However, to neglect to speak also of its potential danger is a dereliction of duty. Jesus and the apostles warned the people of God about many things. Today, some preachers don't seem to warn the Church about much of anything, other than the "blessing" of giving to their particular ministry, and the "curse" if you do not. May ministers of the gospel declare once again like Paul:

I kept back nothing that was profitable unto you…for I have not shunned to declare unto you all the counsel of God…I ceased not to **warn** *every one night and day.* (Acts 20:20, 27, 31)

MAY GOD BLESS AMERICA!

Contact the Author

I would love to hear your comments and/or testimonies about how this book has impacted your life in Christ. You may contact me via email or mail.

Email:

victoryfortoday@aol.com

Phone:

407.296.7131

Mailing Address:

Victorious Living Ministries

P.O. Box 617199

Orlando, Florida 32861

Victorious Living Ministries is available to minister the material covered in this book in your venue, or other topics, which our precious Lord has graciously revealed to the author.

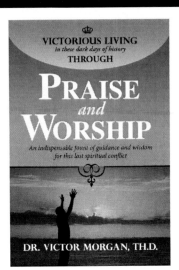
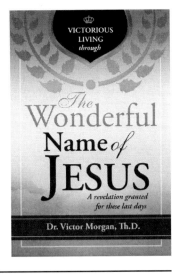
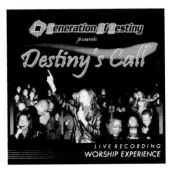